Biblical Sterne

NEW DIRECTIONS IN RELIGION AND LITERATURE

This series aims to showcase new work at the forefront of religion and literature through short studies written by leading and rising scholars in the field. Books will pursue a variety of theoretical approaches as they engage with writing from different religious and literary traditions. Collectively, the series will offer a timely critical intervention to the interdisciplinary crossover between religion and literature, speaking to wider contemporary interests and mapping out new directions for the field in the early twenty-first century.

Series editors: Emma Mason and Mark Knight

ALSO AVAILABLE IN THE SERIES:

The New Atheist Novel, Arthur Bradley and Andrew Tate
Blake. Wordsworth. Religion, Jonathan Roberts
Do the Gods Wear Capes?, Ben Saunders
England's Secular Scripture, Jo Carruthers
Victorian Parables, Susan E. Colón
The Late Walter Benjamin, John Schad
Dante and the Sense of Transgression, William Franke
The Glyph and the Gramophone, Luke Ferretter
John Cage and Buddhist Ecopoetics, Peter Jaeger
Rewriting the Old Testament in Anglo-Saxon Verse, Samantha Zacher
Forgiveness in Victorian Literature, Richard Hughes Gibson
The Gospel According to the Novelist, Magdalena Mączyńska
Jewish Feeling, Richa Dwor
Beyond the Willing Suspension of Disbelief, Michael Tomko
The Gospel According to David Foster Wallace, Adam S. Miller
Pentecostal Modernism, Stephen Shapiro and Philip Barnard
The Bible in the American Short Story, Lesleigh Cushing Stahlberg and Peter S. Hawkins
Faith in Poetry, Michael D. Hurley
Jeanette Winterson and Religion, Emily McAvan
Religion and American Literature since the 1950s, Mark Eaton
Esoteric Islam in Modern French Thought, Ziad Elmarsafy

FORTHCOMING:

Marilynne Robinson's Wordly Gospel, Ryan S. Kemp and Jordan M. Rodgers
Weird Faith in 19th Century Literature, Mark Knight and Emma Mason

Biblical Sterne

Rhetoric and Religion in the Shandyverse

Ryan J. Stark

BLOOMSBURY ACADEMIC
LONDON • NEW YORK • OXFORD • NEW DELHI • SYDNEY

BLOOMSBURY ACADEMIC
Bloomsbury Publishing Plc
50 Bedford Square, London, WC1B 3DP, UK
1385 Broadway, New York, NY 10018, USA
29 Earlsfort Terrace, Dublin 2, Ireland

BLOOMSBURY, BLOOMSBURY ACADEMIC and the Diana logo are
trademarks of Bloomsbury Publishing Plc

First published in Great Britain 2021
Paperback edition published 2022

Copyright © Ryan J. Stark, 2021

Ryan J. Stark has asserted his right under the Copyright, Designs and
Patents Act, 1988, to be identified as Author of this work.

For legal purposes the Acknowledgments on p. vi constitute an
extension of this copyright page.

Cover design by Namkwan Cho

All rights reserved. No part of this publication may be reproduced or
transmitted in any form or by any means, electronic or mechanical,
including photocopying, recording, or any information storage or retrieval
system, without prior permission in writing from the publishers.

Bloomsbury Publishing Plc does not have any control over, or responsibility for,
any third-party websites referred to or in this book. All internet addresses given
in this book were correct at the time of going to press. The author and publisher
regret any inconvenience caused if addresses have changed or sites have
ceased to exist, but can accept no responsibility for any such changes.

A catalogue record for this book is available from the British Library.

Library of Congress Cataloging-in-Publication Data
Names: Stark, Ryan J., author.
Title: Biblical Sterne : rhetoric and religion in the shandyverse / Ryan J. Stark.
Description: London ; New York : Bloomsbury Academic, 2021. |
Series: New directions in religion and literature |
Includes bibliographical references and index.
Identifiers: LCCN 2020040928 (print) | LCCN 2020040929 (ebook) |
ISBN 9781350177789 (hb) | ISBN 9781350202894 (pb) |
ISBN 9781350179998 (epdf) | ISBN 9781350177796 (ebook)
Subjects: LCSH: Sterne, Laurence, 1713-1768–Criticism
and interpretation. | Bible–In literature. | Humor in literature.
Classification: LCC PR3716 .S77 2021 (print) |
LCC PR3716 (ebook) | DDC 823/.6–dc23
LC record available at https://lccn.loc.gov/2020040928
LC ebook record available at https://lccn.loc.gov/2020040929

ISBN: HB: 978-1-3501-7778-9
PB: 978-1-3502-0289-4
ePDF: 978-1-3501-7999-8
eBook: 978-1-3501-7779-6

Series: New Directions in Religion and Literature

Typeset by Integra Software Services Pvt. Ltd.

To find out more about our authors and books visit www.bloomsbury.com
and sign up for our newsletters.

Table of Contents

Acknowledgments		vi
1	The Shandean Apology	1
2	Paranormal *Tristram Shandy*	9
3	Are the Sermons Funny?	29
4	Maria in the Biblical Sense	47
5	Otherworldly Yorick	71
6	Ghost Rhetoric	93
7	Why Sterne?	113
Notes		119
Bibliography		143
Index		168

Acknowledgments

I am deeply grateful to Mark Knight and Emma Mason for believing in this project, and to Ben Doyle for shepherding my book proposal as he did. I thank Lucy Brown, assistant editor, for all her help, the anonymous reviewers for their wisdom, and the copyeditors for their scrutiny. I am thankful, too, for the good humor of many friends and teachers over the years. God bless them all: David Mason, Ted Gracyk, David Myers, Arnold Johanson, Mark Chekola, Susan Woolf, Leroy Meyer, Alan Shepard, Jan Swearingen, Neil Easterbrook, Elizabeth Spiller, Amy Kimme Hea, Melinda Turnley, Piper Murray, Bill Feuer, Desmond Dewsnap, John Holland, Ashley Kunsa, Ashley Marshall, Joseph Pappa, Catherine Kemp, Mitchell Aboulafia, Tina Skouen, Rich Doyle, Jeff Nealon, Rosa Eberly, Kent Kersey, Colette Tennant, Laurie Smith, Allen Jones, Felicia Squires, and Matt Lucas. Much gratitude goes to my family, also, for their loving encouragement: Aaron and Brett, Tanya and Marilyn, nephew Tyler, and my heroic parents—Dennie and Jeanette. Finally, I happily acknowledge the University of Delaware Press, who permitted me to reuse work from my chapter titled "*Tristram Shandy* and the Devil" (2011), and Oxford University Press, who allowed me to reuse work from two articles: "Are Laurence Sterne's Sermons Funny?" (*Literature and Theology*, 2015) and "Sterne's Maria in the Biblical Sense" (*The Cambridge Quarterly*, 2016).

1

The Shandean Apology

The problem with pornography is not that it shows too much of the person, Pope John Paul II observed, but that it shows far too little.[1] I have yet to find evidence that John Paul had Laurence Sterne on the desk when he made this insightful point, but I would like to imagine that he did. We discover in the Shandyverse the same idea. Sterne presents it differently, of course, and in a manner unsettling for those who cling too tightly to decorum, but he and the Pope arrive at equivalent sentimental conclusions: they know we have souls and that the pornographer's single entendres bear false witness against the dignity of personhood. Here, then, is the first hallmark of the Shandean apology, and perhaps the most technical from a rhetorical standpoint: the double entendre, if marshalled correctly, protects human beings against lurid superficiality. Real smut welcomes simplicity, as does real religious fundamentalism, Enlightenment rationalism, logical positivism, or any other grave monomania expressed through the framework of a plain rhetoric. On the contrary, Sterne's suggestive wordplay functions in exactly the opposite way, certainly connecting the verities of life to the sexual impulse, but also—and just as certainly—connecting the sexual impulse to the verities of life. They are mixed and for the great satirist held in precarious balance. The absence of that balance is what Sterne confronts on the rhetorical level with his Shandean banter.

From where Sterne developed this knack for sexual innuendo is a separate question. Typically, critics point first to Rabelais and Shakespeare, but mention also Cervantes, Erasmus, Burton, and Swift, among others. This is perfectly good company in which to place Sterne, but behind these figures lies a much older source from which he drew, that is, the Bible, wherein Sterne first discovered Shandean possibilities. Note, for example, that Old Testament Hebrew contains no word for "penis," though euphemisms for the virile member abound, including "the virile member," "foot," "finger," "thigh," "hollow socket," as in Jacob's "hollow socket," "key," and "rib." The last might interest those who have wondered about Adam's rib in the Septuagint and, relatedly, why the human male conspicuously lacks a baculum.[2] As Yorick reminds us in the *Journey*, the shopkeeper's wife is the bone of the shopkeeper's bone.[3] Nor do the authors of holy writ leave un-euphemized the feminine counterpart: "bowl," "keyhole," "form," as in Isaiah 3:17's exposed "form," "shoe," and "hand," to name a few, and the "palms" of the hands in the case of Jezebel's durable palms.[4] They remained stubbornly intact even after the horses trampled her to death and the dogs ran away with most of her body.[5] Rabelais—we might remember—reinvents the Jezebel scene in the form of Friar Tickletoby's demise, the licentious priest who also suffers a death-by-horse-trampling scenario, with only his severed "foot" surviving as evidence of the ordeal.[6] And from Rabelais to Sterne, where Tristram bouncily flirts with the curious female reader who, if tempted by a devilish thought, is told "to jump it, to rear it, to bound it," and, if necessary, "to kick it"—just "like Tickletoby's mare."[7] Sage advice, no doubt, or maybe an indecent proposal. Maybe both.

All of this is to say that Sterne comes honestly by his penchant for sexual innuendo, from noses and knee rubs to buttonholes and petticoats; from Elisha and the Shunammite woman recast as Yorick and Mrs. Shandy, for example, to the Pentateuch's immodest lady wrestler reconfigured as Tom's sausage-making-Jewish-widow girlfriend, who inspires one of the best of all Shandean adages: "There is nothing so awkward, as courting a woman, an' please your honour, whilst she is making sausages."[8] Presumably, too, those inquisitive readers of Scripture will recall the lady wrestler's punishment for grabbing a man by the genitals. It is commanded in Deuteronomy

25:12 that her hand be cut off, or that she endure a total bikini wax, depending on how one translates the passage.[9] The latter—the bikini wax tribulation—is the more Christian of the two punishments, I believe, and certainly the more Shandean.

One gets the impression that the Reverend Joseph Cockfield understood these matters in some detail, when, after pouring over Sterne and pondering the Bible, he queried, "Who that indulges serious reflection can read [Sterne's] obscenity and ill-applied passages of Holy Scripture without horror?"[10] We arrive, then, at the second hallmark of the Shandean apology: an irreverently reverent use of Scripture in the service of satire, often risqué in nature. Not coincidentally, this second hallmark abruptly leads to a third, which is the upsetting of overly sensitive Christians, who are the primary target of Sterne's wit, not counting the Devil. And the provocations worked. That is, Sterne upset a lot of Christians, the moral busybodies, in particular. The Goodman Browns. The Mrs. Grundys. He had a knack for it. John Wesley strongly urged against reading Sterne, for instance, unless one prefers "uncouthness," in which case he is "without rival."[11] The Presbyterian minister Samuel Miller described *Tristram* as "shamefully obscene," while the Anglican priest Vicemus Knox—writing in the late eighteenth century—deemed Sterne "the grand promoter of adultery, and [of] every species of illicit commerce," before pinning upon him England's rising divorce rate.[12] Indeed, we could find an inordinate number of additional examples. Politicians, self-appointed cultural critics, the publisher Ralph Griffiths, who declared Sterne a "pimp to every lewd idea," and the moralizer "D. Whyte," who enquired, "Must a clergyman of the Church of England set himself up as a second Satan?"[13] Famously, too, the abolitionist William Wilberforce disapproved, calling Sterne "indecent" and with "pernicious purposes," a writer "eminently culpable" for "corrupting the national taste" and "lowering the standard of manners and morals" everywhere.[14] He said this, it should be noted, while standing on Sterne's shoulders, heavily indebted to the Shandyverse's daring abolitionist rhetoric.[15] One could say that without Sterne there would be no Wilberforce, which might not ring entirely true, but nor does it ring false. On how the genial Sterne managed to elicit so many expressions of outrage, theories will undoubtedly vary, but the psychological condition motivating the outrage might very well be the same across the board. As Arthur Cash discerned, "There is less excuse for those literary critics and conceited moralists whose only aim has been to suppress the frivolity they cannot share."[16]

Not all is doom and gloom, however. Sterne also gathered admirers, and continues to do so, many of whom are far afield from the usual readers of Christian literature. This brings us to the fourth and—for our purposes—final hallmark of the Shandean apology, that is, to share mirth with the David Humes and Friedrich Nietzsches of the world. The latter—of "God is dead" fame—praised Sterne as the freest spirit to have ever lived, a sentiment largely shared by Goethe and Schopenhauer, neither of whom attended church regularly.[17] Hume, the man who said that "supernatural beliefs" had been "everywhere rejected by men of sense," thought *Tristram Shandy* the best English book of the mid-eighteenth century, and thought Sterne an orthodox Anglican priest.[18] After cutting-and-pasting together his own version of the Bible, the deist Thomas Jefferson called Sterne's writings "the best course on morality ever written," while Abraham Lincoln, possibly America's first bisexual president, comically quoted the *Journey*'s starling anecdote as he pondered his own circumstances in the presidency: "I can't get out!"[19] And then we discover Virginia Woolf, whose admiration for Sterne is well documented, as is her now-infamous response to the happy news of T.S. Eliot's conversion: "I have had a most shameful and distressing interview with poor dear Tom Eliot, who may be called dead to us all from this day forward. He has become an Anglo-Catholic, believes in God and immortality, and goes to church."[20]

In the history of Christian apologetics, one is hard-pressed to find another figure who elicits such a curious collection of replies. What kind of Christian apologist finds such obvious comradery with the twin pillars of modern atheism and such palpable friction with so many prominent religious luminaries, if not full-blown excommunication from them? The best kind, I think, to answer the question forthright, and certainly the Shandean kind, which brings me to my overarching theme: Sterne advances the Christian faith in a decidedly odd way and against the better judgment of gloomy religionists everywhere. Of course, such a thesis may sound like old news to Herbert Read, who—in 1937—pointed out that Sterne's fictions and sermons put forward the same Christian arguments, in essence, one implicitly and the other explicitly.[21] This is also what Sterne meant, most likely, when he described *Tristram Shandy* as "a moral work, more read than understood," and is, too, the convincing line of criticism taken by Cash, Melvyn New, Stephen Prickett, and Elizabeth Kraft, among others, that is, a religious Sterne making religious claims.[22] Allow me therefore a slight emendation to my theme, given that I run the risk of stating the obvious: Sterne defends the Christian faith in a manner even stranger and more mischievous than is currently understood, by a long way, I think, and for reasons that are a pleasure to explain. Gwendolyn—from Oscar Wilde's *The Importance of Being Earnest*—prefaces one of her speeches as follows: "On an occasion of this kind, it becomes more than a moral duty to speak one's mind. It becomes a pleasure."[23] Such is my preface as well.

I divide this book into five chapters, not counting the introduction and conclusion, and organize them chronologically, with the caveat that *The Sermons of Mr. Yorick* were drafted before *Tristram Shandy*, or at least mostly drafted, but were not attributed to "Yorick" until after Sterne had invented the Shandyverse. Ergo, I think it best to imagine Sterne and Yorick as co-authors of the homilies, which causes me to place them after *Tristram Shandy*.

In Chapter 2, "Paranormal *Tristram Shandy*," I argue that Sterne exorcises the real Devil from the bedeviled mind of writer and reader alike, not the fake Devil of the modern literary imagination. Sterne performs an "exorcism, most unecclesiastically," and does it primarily through humor, taking very much to heart Thomas More's observation that "the Devil ... the proud spirit ... cannot endure to be mocked."[24] And if the real Satan is the Shandyverse's arch villain, then other implications follow as well, not least of which is the thought that Ephesians 6:12 proves more important than John Locke to understanding Tristram's psychology: "For we wrestle not against flesh and blood, but against principalities, against powers, against the rulers of the darkness of this world, against spiritual wickedness in high places."

In the third chapter, "Are the Sermons Funny?," I reopen a seemingly closed debate, arguing against the modern critics that the sermons do—indeed—carry a Shandean tint. Not that they are impious or in any way unsuitable for the pulpit. Nevertheless, Sterne amuses, and some of the humor is risqué and requires more than a passing knowledge of Scripture to appreciate. This last point once more highlights a neglected but crucial source of inspiration for Sterne's comic genius: the Bible, especially the Old Testament, that ancient repository of wisdom and proto-Shandean intrigue.

In Chapter 4, I revisit the Maria of Moulins scenes, one in *Tristram* and the other in the *Journey*. I argue that both allude to Genesis 38. Maria plays the role of Tamar, while Tristram and Yorick step into variations upon the role of Judah. The episodes are counterfactual insofar as Maria fails to get pregnant, but the overall moral of the Maria scenes is very much in line with the scriptural admonition against overconfidence, especially as it relates to how we imagine ourselves able to resist temptation. Cases in point: Tristram and Yorick set out with perfectly good intensions, I show, but when confronted by real temptation, that is, a convenient prostitute, their delicacy quickly turns to concupiscence.

In the final chapters, 5 and 6, I explain why Sterne conjures up Yorick's ghost and sends him to France. Specifically, I argue that Sterne uses the fleshy ghost to critique Gnostic and atheistic attitudes toward life. A sentimental ghost story, probably the first of its kind, the *Journey* demonstrates God's mercy beyond the grave, giving full literary credence to that mysterious passage in 1 Peter where we hear of Christ preaching to the dead: "For this cause was the gospel preached also to those who are dead, that they might be judged according to men in the flesh, but live according to God in the spirit."[25] The Dogberrian philosopher Yogi Berra once observed, "It ain't over till it's over."[26] Sterne's implicit Shandean proverb in the *Journey* bears a family resemblance: it is not over even when it is over, as is evidenced by Yorick's final theosis, which ends as all things end on this side of Heaven, not at the end but rather with a particularly dramatic aposiopesis.

And perhaps it goes without saying that laughter is the dominant side effect of the Shandean apology. True laughter. The sort of laughter about which the demon Screwtape complains because it disrupts "the realism, dignity, and austerity of Hell."[27] A second side effect often follows, which is the development of tenderness, a disposition also mixed with nostalgia, romance, and love for the neighbor. If read correctly, Sterne provokes such feelings, regardless of one's theological commitments—or lack thereof. Finally, on a concluding note, Sterne's Christian rhetoric prompts something else unexpected in many of us, a third side effect, and this is a renewed curiosity about Scripture, insofar as few writers have recuperated the Bible's strangeness in the way Sterne has. If, in fact, Sterne's style is a consequence of his daily Bible devotions, which he said it was, and I believe him, then the Bible must be a very odd book indeed.[28] To put a finer point on the matter: Samuel

Johnson had forgotten the Bible's oddity when he declared that "nothing odd will do long."[29] In a different era and on a different continent, Flannery O'Connor did not forget: alluding to John 8:32, she arrived at the heart of a truism about biblically informed Christianity and therefore, by logical extension, a truism about Sterne's biblically informed Christianity: "You shall know the truth, and the truth shall make you odd."[30]

2

Paranormal *Tristram Shandy*

The Devil frequently appears in *Tristram Shandy*. Old Nick.[1] Old Harry. Old Gooseberry. He is "the great disturber of our faiths in this world," Tristram reminds us, and "he never lies dead in a ditch."[2] Throughout the book, we confront "temptations and suggestions of the devil," not to mention suspicions about him: for example, "*Ferdinand de Cordouè* was so wise at nine," we are told, "'twas thought the devil was in him;—and at *Venice* gave such proofs of his knowledge and goodness, that the monks imagined he was *Antichrist*."[3] An early reviewer imagined that Sterne was Antichrist, but for different reasons.[4] And it is not only The Enemy per se who accounts for *Tristram*'s preternatural atmosphere, but also the "FIFTY thousand pannier loads of devils," the "imps, with their hammers and engines," and the "little party-colour'd devils."[5] Tristram alludes to Satan and his horde more frequently than he does to John Locke, or to anyone else for that matter, save the other main characters.[6] The "arch-jockey of jockeys" sits not exactly at the center of the Shandyverse, but rather runs alongside—and perhaps astride—nearly every notable scene.[7] And even when he is not there, he is there, as in the case of the nuns who try to move their mule up a hill by using half-profane language:

> Quicker still, cried Margarita.
> Fou, fou, fou, fou, fou, fou, fou, fou, fou.
> Quicker still, cried Margarita.
> Bou, bou, bou, bou, bou, bou, bou, bou.
> Quicker still—God preserve me! Said the abbess—They do not understand us, cried Margarita—But the Devil does, said the abbess of Andoüillets.[8]

Coleridge saw all of this and decided that Sterne dallied with the Devil, which is as unlikely as the claim that Milton dallied with the Devil in *Paradise Lost*.[9] But that Sterne shows an unusual preoccupation with demonry seems abundantly clear. Why? To what end? Does he invent gothic fiction before Horace Walpole? Are we to read *Tristram Shandy* as an eccentric commentary on Ephesians 6:12—our struggle is not against flesh and blood but against wicked spirits in heavenly places? Or is it that Sterne performs an "exorcism, most unecclesiastically," by drawing to the surface and then lampooning our many demonic thoughts, a comic version of the *Thesaurus Exorcismorum*?[10] The answer to all of these questions is yes, I believe, and emphatically so to the last one.

Tristram Shandy is a comic exorcism, a cathartic ritual by which writer and readers alike laugh away the Devil, as Martin Luther advised we must, if the Devil "will not yield to texts of Scripture."[11] Tristram, our flawed protagonist, stands in for all who find themselves overwhelmed by their own material. He zigzags his way through life's riddles and mysteries, resisting temptation, at least at times, and mourning with those in the house of mourning, but never at the expense of a good joke, which proves crucial if he—and we—are to rebuff Hell's incessant gravity. Of course, *Tristram Shandy* is many other things as well: a satire, a novel, a satire upon the novel.[12] It is, most agree, a book for free spirits, and also—as Bishop Warburton warned—not to be read in the company of those who easily faint.[13] Sterne's persistent talk of devilry, however, reminds us of another dimension, and this a neglected one: the paranormal. Seldom do critics point to *Tristram*'s occult sensibility, but we are hard-pressed to describe it otherwise, once we comprehend the allusions to demons and principalities. Sterne brings us closer to the ghost episodes from *Hamlet*, or the weird-sister scenes from *Macbeth*, than to the afternoon conversations among the philosophers, but with a crucial caveat: Shandean humor. Sterne amuses, not to downplay the preternatural atmosphere, as some might think, but rather to demonstrate for believers and seekers alike how best to engage the Devil, when the Devil knocks at the door. Herein we discover the deepest rationale for Sterne's spiritual comedy, the religious rationale, that is, to cast out demons through the unceremonious liturgy of redemptive laughter. Who better than Sterne to guide such a processional?

Sterne's Demonological Framework

In 1604, in canon 72, the Church of England forbade any priest to perform exorcisms without a license from the bishop. To quote the source, priests were not "without such License to attempt upon any pretense whatsoever whether of possession or obsession, by fasting or prayer, to cast out any devil or devils, under pain of the imputation of Imposture, or Cozenage, and Deposition from the Ministry."[14] No licenses were ever issued, and yet—unsurprisingly—clandestine procedures continued throughout the early modern period, and beyond, along with steady reports of demonic activity.[15] Most people living in North Yorkshire County, and everywhere else in Christendom, believed in the Devil. They accepted the idea that Satan influenced people either directly through possession or indirectly, and far more commonly, by other means: bewitchments, fascinations, dreams, dangerous books. Thomas Hobbes was outlier, in other words, when he rejected demonry on the ground that possessions were simply cases of madness misunderstood.[16] The problem, he argued, was not in metaphysics but rather in nomenclature. Nor would the conversation about Hell between James Boswell and Lord Kames have garnered widespread agreement a century after Hobbes. Boswell told Kames that the idea of Hell's torments harmed the world, to which Kames dismissively replied, "Nobody believes it."[17] By "nobody," he meant himself and a few urbane colleagues, not the vast majority of thinkers who lived in the Age of Reason, or what others have called—with equal justification—the Age of Theosophy.[18]

Much closer to the period's mainstream understanding was William Whiston, successor to Newton in the Lucasian Chair of Mathematics at Cambridge. He argued that the idea of demonic influence was "no more to be denied" than "Mr. Boyle's experiments about the elasticity of the air, or Sir Isaac Newton's demonstrations about the power of gravity," insofar as all involved invisible forces that nonetheless left marks on the material world.[19] Like every good scientist, Whiston preferred evidence, and from the evidence concluded that some demonic possessions were real, even if not entirely explicable, while others were false. Essentially, Whiston restated for an Enlightenment audience Thomas Browne's well-known verdict in *Religio Medici* (1642): "The devil doth really possess some men; the spirit of melancholy others; the spirit of delusion others."[20] The task therefore is to distinguish among these spirits, a point supremely illustrated in *Hamlet*, for instance, where the prince, upon encountering his father's ghost, rightly wonders if he sees an actual ghost, a "goblin damn'd," or a grief-born hallucination.[21] If one has a strict doctrine against the existence of demons and ghosts, then the natural explanation is the only one to be entertained, obviously, just as the non-miraculous account is the only account for a miracle, if one accepts David Hume's preemptive doctrine against miracles.[22] But for most philosophers in Sterne's era, and certainly for all orthodox clergy, the wise course of action was not proactively to deny the possibility of demonic influence but rather to "test the spirits" per 1 John 4:1, after which a diagnosis might be made. Indeed, this has always been the wise course of action within a traditional Christian framework, Sterne's framework included.

How, then, does Sterne perceive the Devil? We discover in his works competing attitudes. Walter most cogently presents the skeptical position, describing the Devil as a useful but mere allegory, a "poetic fiction" invented to condemn the world's tartufferies.[23] That is, Walter disbelieves, a point Tristram promises to explain more fully than he ever does, in what amounts to another of the Shandyverse's many loose ends. For the clearest counterstatement to Walter's position, we discover Yorick, not only in *Tristram*, where he expectedly demonstrates the worldview of a traditional Anglican priest, but also—and more dramatically—in the *Journey*, when, in the "Temptation" scene, he picks up a pen, puts it down, trembles, and then declares that the Devil is in him, by which he means the Devil, not an antiquated metaphor, nor a chimera of the primitive imagination. And while Tristram's position is slightly less certain than Yorick's, given that Tristram never reports a possession, he nonetheless confirms his belief in supernatural realities, devils and all. He does this in two ways, first by sincerely alluding to otherworldly forces throughout the satire, and, second, by playfully regretting that some of his readers disbelieve, with the hope that they will not lay the blame for their disbelief at his feet, given all the bawdy banter that threatens to disrupt the pilgrims on their pilgrimages.[24]

Somewhere intermingled among these characters is Sterne himself, whose position is best understood as nearly synonymous with Yorick's, if not entirely so. For Sterne, the Devil is the Devil, with one of the strongest indicators appearing in a candid letter to his friend John Hall-Stevenson, where he addresses his own struggle with infidelity: "I do not know what is the matter with me, but I am sick and tired of my wife more than ever—and I am possessed by a Devil who drives me to town."[25] Sterne does not refer to a figurative Devil, here, nor to a bland abstraction, shared witticism, or whatever else might be said in an effort to explain away the existential reality of Satan. Rather, he recounts the extent to which an external force nudges him toward an action he would not otherwise take, or would not otherwise want to take, to recall Paul's self-admonition in Romans 7:19: "For I do not do the good I want, but the evil I do not want is what I do." Not that Sterne avoids culpability with his devil-made-me-do-it excuse, or even wants to avoid culpability. The opposite is the case: he bluntly presents his own guilt in this letter. The point to be made, however, is not about guilt but rather discernment, and, more specifically, Sterne's discernment that he had preternatural company on his ride to town. Sterne acknowledges the Devil's presence, which makes him something other than the secular humanist Martin Battestin imagined him to be.[26]

In the sermons, too, we discover remarks that confirm Sterne's orthodox position. Indeed, he often mentions the demonic realm, either straightforwardly or obliquely, but nowhere more convincingly than in the "Temporal Advantages of Religion," where he pinpoints Satan's oldest rhetorical gambit against human beings: "As the deceiver of mankind thus began his triumph over our race—so has he carried it on ever since by the very same argument of delusion.—That is, by possessing men's minds early with great expectations of the present incomes of sin."[27] We have no reason to suppose that Sterne—with this talk of devilry—denotes anything other than the real Devil. We should take him at his word. And if not here, then in the sermon on the Levite and his concubine, for example, where he observes that satire of the deeply bitter sort, if it is to be called satire at all, is a special talent of the Devil. Or in the sermon on peace, where Sterne cogently presents the three enemies of the soul, as Peter Abelard labeled them: the world, the flesh, and the Devil, with the caveat that the Devil is to be understood in the traditional sense, however barbaric the thought might be to Baron d'Holbach and his salon of atheists. Various other sermons illustrate the same basic idea, predictably, and there is—in addition to the sermonic evidence—a simple deductive argument to be noted. If Sterne is a traditional priest with a traditional view of Scripture, theologically speaking, then we simply cannot avoid Satan, and nor can we avoid the biblical fact that Christ exorcised devils on at least five occasions, the most dramatic of which appears in Matthew 8:28-34, where Jesus casts a legion of demons into a herd of pigs. In one of Scripture's truly proto-Shandean moments, the pigs then rush into the sea and drown themselves, to the disgruntlement of the herd's owner, presumably, and the terror of the townspeople, who—rather than thanking Christ—entreat him to leave the region immediately.[28] Serious exorcisms tend to upset onlookers, as it happens, and comic exorcisms, too.

In short, we do ourselves and Sterne a disservice if we mythologize what is so obviously a forthright theme in his letters, sermons, and fiction: the Devil tempts us often and to great effect. The Devil cajoles us, just as he "and all the devils in hell" cajoled John de la Casa, the priest who thought that Satan took an exceptional interest in distinguished religious men.[29] And by "Satan," de la Casa, Tristram, Yorick, and Sterne point to that same defiant presence in the universe who seeks our ruin. Mr. Scratch. The Prince of this World, as John the Apostle describes him. The Father of Curses.[30] Behind all these titles is the basic Christian perception that we find ourselves in a cosmic struggle between good and evil, and that evil—like goodness—has a real presence.

Unsentimental Satan

A paranormal ambience pervades *Tristram Shandy*, but perhaps nowhere more dramatically than in the sentimental crescendos, three of which are of particular interest: Toby and the fly, Le Fever's death, and the address to Jenny in the last volume. In each, we encounter an allusion to the demonic, as the barrier between the natural and the preternatural subsides, allowing us to see more clearly the occult framework in which Sterne forwards his comic apology.

First, to Toby and the fly, one of the Shandyverse's most misunderstood episodes:

> Go,—says he, one day at dinner, to an over-grown one which had buzz'd about his nose, and tormented him cruelly all dinner-time,—and which, after infinite attempts, he had caught at last, as it flew by him;—I'll not hurt thee, says my uncle *Toby*, rising from

his chair, and going a-cross the room, with the fly in his hand,—I'll not hurt a hair of thy head:—Go, says he, lifting up the sash, and opening his hand as he spoke, to let it escape;—go poor Devil, get thee gone, why should I hurt thee?—This world surely is wide enough to hold both thee and me.[31]

Toby's reference to "poor Devil" hardly seems pregnant with meaning. It reads instead like a thoughtless and colloquial apostrophe, though we should suspect otherwise. Sterne has a light touch at times, but he also likes to hide things in plain sight. In this case, he uses "poor Devil" to disguise the obvious by flaunting it, much as he does with the reference to "the duce" in Walter's acknowledgment that he cannot imagine "who the duce" Tristram takes after: Yorick, Mrs. Shandy, and the Devil make three.[32] Specifically, Sterne—through Toby's "poor Devil" reference—cleverly retells the Ahaziah story from 2 Kings 1. Here, one of Israel's worst kings, after damaging his groin, sends messengers to the Philistine city of Ekron to ask Beelzebub, Lord of the Flies, if and when he will heal: "Go inquire of Beelzebub, the god of Ekron, whether I shall recover from this injury."[33] That the king did not seek Yahweh's council displeased Yahweh, we are told, and thus Ahaziah never heals, dying a wounded man—unable to get past his injury. The same can be said of uncle Toby, who also never heals from his wound, as suggested most pertinently by his failed courtship with the Widow Wadman.

But the more important point for our purpose is that Toby, also exactly like Ahaziah, shows too much deference to Beelzebub, not only in the homage to the fly, but also in his response to Dr. Slop's reading of Ernulphus's curse, which gives us a fuller sense of Toby's sentimental attitude toward Satan:

> I declare, quoth my uncle *Toby*, my heart would not let me curse the devil himself with so much bitterness.—He is the father of curses, replied Dr. *Slop*.—So am not I, replied my uncle.—But he is cursed, and damn'd already, to all eternity,—replied Dr. *Slop*. I am sorry for it, quoth my uncle *Toby*.[34]

The man of feeling is one thing, and the man of feeling toward the Devil another. Toby is of the latter sort, and as such demonstrates how unrestrained sentimentality in an age of conscience might subtly curve in on itself and become a vice, not a virtue.[35] The wrong sentiment toward hazardous things proves hazardous, in other words, a point seemingly beyond Toby's immediate grasp, largely because he imagines a ceasefire with the Devil. But, as it happens, the world is not wide enough for Toby and the pestilence. Beelzebub always returns. There is no peace to be bargained, or truce to be made, though Satan would have us believe otherwise.

The matter of Toby and Beelzebub never found its way into the criticism, probably because the scene appeared early on in the hugely successful *Beauties of Sterne* (1782), under the category of "Mercy"— of which Toby shows much.[36] He demonstrates other laudable characteristics as well, not least of which is his compassion toward the downtrodden. Almost from the start, therefore, Toby became emblematic of venerable sentimentality, an example of Shandean high-mindedness. Alongside this positive image, however, we discover a neglected and much darker cautionary note, if we have ears to hear. That is, Sterne—through Toby's self-deception and naïveté— cautions us not to give an inch to the Devil. Or, to recall a wise medieval proverb, "he who sups with that formidable host needs a long spoon."[37]

A demon more obviously appears in Le Fever's death scene, where Toby, in a moment of poignant denial, swears by God that the lieutenant will not die, which triggers a pro forma demonic response:

—He shall not die, by G—, cried my uncle *Toby*.
—The accusing spirit which flew up to heaven's chancery with the oath, blush'd as he gave it in;—and the recording angel as he wrote it down, dropp'd a tear upon the word, and blotted it out for ever.[38]

The episode alludes to the book of Deeds from Revelation 20:12, as New notes, but Tristram also refers explicitly and more importantly to Isaiah 43:25, where God declares, "I, even I, am he that blotteth out thy transgressions for mine own sake, and will not remember thy sins."[39] Other verses suggest much the same, Psalm 51:9 and Acts 3:19, for example, where we discover that God has a smudging effect on the book of Deeds, making any quantitative approach to sinning highly problematic. Put differently, God forgives and forgets, as the crying angel demonstrates, but the scene also comes with an interpretive temptation worth exploring. Why does the Accusing Spirit blush with embarrassment as he reports Toby's oath in the first place, Toby's swearing by God's name in vain? Given that devils have a reputation for not blushing, ever, the blush here invites us to see the demon as a sensitive soul, a fiend with a soft side who presumably knows that the sin in this context, if it is a sin at all, is to be expected; the demon is surely not surprised by Toby's "By G—," but nor does he seem delighted. Indeed, we are tempted to perceive in the devil a sense of relief when the angel behaves mercifully, and seemingly behind God's back. On such a reading, the demon blushes out of shame for an inflexible God, or shame for a legalistic theology that buries believers in technicalities and unreasonable expectations. And of such religions there is no end. But Tristram's reference to Isaiah 43:25 changes everything, making the demon-is-embarrassed-on-behalf-of-Christianity interpretation both difficult and undesirable. The blush is much better explained, instead, by the devil's desperate behavior coupled with his inability to hide the desperation. By trying to indict uncle Toby, he grasps at straws, and on some instinctive level detects his own foolishness in making the accusation. That is, the war on Heaven goes poorly, and the blush reveals to us that the demon catches a glimpse in the mirror of his own ragged visage. The scene's sentimentality, therefore, has little to do with a meeting of the minds between two spirits, one good and one evil. We do not find ourselves as witnesses to a brief marriage of Heaven and Hell. Rather, what Sterne demonstrates is God's always-present inclination toward grace, which brings with it also—somewhere in the scene's background music—a hint that there will be justice in the next life, if not this one. Such is the Christian promise to all who cope with loss, Toby included, that no loss goes unnoticed, that no loss is in vain.

Last, to the Jenny address, or to the argument that precedes it, where Tristram thinks about his own work contra Swift and Warburton: "for what has [*Tristram Shandy*] done more than the *Legation of Moses*, or the *Tale of a Tub*, that it may not swim down the gutter of Time along with them?" Before Tristram defends his book's merits, however, he cannot help but digress, having suddenly become aware of time's passing, and thus preemptively sets aside the foreshadowed debate about what constitutes great writing:

> I will not argue the matter: Time wastes too fast: every letter I trace tells me with what rapidity Life follows my pen; the days and hours of it, more precious, my dear Jenny! than the rubies about thy neck, are flying over our heads like light clouds of a windy day, never to return more—every thing presses on—whilst thou art twisting that lock,—see! it grows grey; and every time I kiss thy hand to bid adieu, and every absence which follows it, are preludes to that eternal separation which we are shortly to make.—
> —Heaven have mercy upon us both![40]

Time does waste too fast. What intensifies this epiphany, however, is not the ticking of the clock but rather Tristram's unexpected reference to "eternal separation," a phrase that carries a quite negative undertone. It is not the "Prayer" sermon's "eternal inheritance," for example, which is how Sterne characterizes salvation.[41] Nor is it volume 7's rich green plain, where Tristram dances with Nanette and dreams of going to "heaven." On the contrary, "eternal separation" recalls Revelation 20:10 and 21:8, verses on the second death, if not also Mathew 25:41, where Christ sends the damned to "everlasting fire."[42] And neither is this the first time Tristram brings us down such dark pathways: "The Popish doctors," we discover in volume 4, made it plain that Luther was destined to die "cursing and blaspheming," sailing "into the lake of hell fire" via the wind of his own rhetoric.[43] Lessius, Tristram tells us in volume 7, calculated that "one Dutch mile, cubically multiplied, will allow room enough, and to spare, for eight hundred thousand millions, which he supposed to be as great a number of souls (counting from the fall of Adam) as can possibly be damn'd to the end of the world."[44] But these last remarks are parodies of scholastic Hell theory, some of the book's blackest comedy, making Tristram's heartfelt articulation of damnation anxiety all the more noticeable in the Jenny scene.

And had Sterne ended the Jenny address here, full of dread, then we would have an entirely different episode, a *No Exit Tristram Shandy*. But rather than surrendering the scene to an apocalyptic reverie, priestly Sterne, in a moment of theological virtuosity, has it so that Tristram prays: "Heav'n have mercy on both of us!" A sudden ejaculation, and it fundamentally changes the atmosphere, because we hear in it the thief on the cross from Luke 23:42, who cries out, "Jesus, remember me when you come into your kingdom." Tired, nostalgic, overwhelmed by his own storytelling, Tristram makes the same desperate gesture. He cries out before God and thus reinforces the work's overall argument that divine grace is the only true remedy for our brokenness. We cannot fix ourselves, and the Great Instauration's new technologies will also fail to deliver us from evil: the innovative forceps, the Tristrapedias. What, then, can we do? We can fall seven times a day, as Sterne reminds us in his sermon on pride, and we can petition Heaven, a simple message from a decidedly complicated book, and one that fundamentally undercuts E.M. Forster's quip about Sterne's first masterpiece: "A god is hidden in *Tristram Shandy*, his name is Muddle, and some readers cannot accept him."[45] That there is a God in *Tristram Shandy* we should not doubt, and manifold devils as well. That this God is Muddle, however, misses the mark, and by missing so badly confirms that the interpretive problem is likely not in accepting Sterne's haphazardness, but rather in accepting his Christianity.

The eighteenth-century poet William Cowper noted that Sterne was "a great master of the pathetic; and if that or any other species of rhetoric could renew the human heart and turn it from the power of Satan unto God," he knew of "no better writer qualified to make proselytes to the cause of virtue."[46] Sadly, however, the compliment is backhanded, because Cowper goes on in the same paragraph to suggest that no species of rhetoric can renew the human heart, an absurd remark for those of us who take comfort in great literature, or who understand what Luther meant when he described the Holy Spirit as the greatest rhetorician of all.[47] That said, Cowper—unlike Forster—gets one ontological point absolutely right: he places the question of Sterne's wit in its proper theological–apologetical–paranormal framework, that is, the spiritual conflict between God and Satan.

Occult Icons

Like the book's sentimental crescendos, the black, marbled, and blank pages also point to spiritual realities, but differently. To use a religious phrasing, they function as icons, enigmatic, séance-like, prompting attentive readers to contemplate the depths of the supernatural, which—in the Shandyverse—tends to be a mixed affair. In volume 3, for example, Tristram calls the black page "the black one," a conventional nomenclature for the Devil, as in "bo melas" from the *Epistle of Barnabas*.[48] Not that the page is emblematic of Satan, but we have reason to believe that a dark energy lurks somewhere in the darkness, that Abaddon lingers. Another clue might be found in volume 5, where Tristram connects the blackness to acts of malice, which fatally wounded Yorick and, in a thinly veiled autobiographical sense, also wounded Sterne.[49] Exactly what else lies "mystically hid under the dark veil" remains a point of some conjecture, but we can easily imagine more gloom.[50] Tristram no doubt hears the persistent derogatory chatter in town that blackens Yorick's remembrance, and he endures the vapid inkhorn rhetoric at Yorick's tombstone, the rehearsals of *Hamlet*'s graveyard speech by bad actors who are only slightly acquainted with the gentle priest and the Bard of Avon. Add to these problems Walter's off-stage cuttlefish eloquence on various aspects of Tristram's breeches, and we arrive at a place of multilayered rhetorical darkness. But like everything else Shandean, there is a superb twist. The black page also amuses, macabre humor in this case, which disrupts any desire for a purely somber mood. Using the blackness, Sterne foreshadows his own demise and comically portends the interpretive confusion surrounding his Rabelaisian wit.[51] Much like the graveyard scene in *Hamlet*, the black page borders upon the slapstick, irreverently mocking death's sting, all the while acknowledging it. We might therefore connect the humor to Thomas More in the tower, for example, who prayed and wrote bawdry while awaiting his execution. And if we look for modern analogues to the black page's gallows humor, we discover—for instance—Spike Mulligan's memorable epitaph, "I told you I was ill," or, better still, Oscar Wilde's pitch-perfect rejoinder: "Either those curtains go or I do."[52] Such also is the force of Sterne's deathbed impertinence.

Overall, the black page demonstrates what James Joyce meant when he said, "I am trying to build as many planes of narrative [as possible] with a single esthetic purpose. Did you ever read Laurence Sterne?"[53] But how many planes of narrative intersect under the dark veil? If we believe Wilbur Cross that Sterne got the idea from Robert Fludd's *Utriusque Cosmi* (1617), which also has a black page, then the answer might be twenty-two, the number of tiers Fludd postulates in his metaphysical coil, stretching from the mushrooms to the angels in a pattern that looks a lot like Trim's swirling stick.[54] Regardless, what we know for certain is that Sterne neither aims at nor achieves the one-dimensional rhetoric sought after by the faux sages in Swift's Laputa, men who communicate using objects, not words, lest they be misunderstood (e.g., ladles, cucumbers, slabs of marble). Nor does he limit himself to the dim literalism of Robert Ferguson, who—in *The Interest of Reason and Religion* (1675)—proclaims, "No Text hath any more than one determinate Sense, otherwise it could have no sense at all."[55] On the contrary, Tristram's veil produces meaningfulness in multiple layers, reminding us of the world beyond our world, memorializing old friends, and—perhaps most significantly—inviting the kind of prophetic laughter that will at the end of time shatter the gates of Hell.

If the black page is the most occult of the three iconic pages, then the marbled page runs a close second, but where, exactly, is the paranormal in this "motley emblem" of Tristram's motley story?[56] Perhaps the best way to find Sterne's occult sensibility here is to search for the biblical scene to which the marble alludes. This may seem provisional as a method, but we should keep in mind that Sterne refers to more than one thousand biblical passages in his sermons, and in the fiction editors have so far discovered more than five hundred scriptural allusions.[57] There are more to discover, including in the marbled page a loud echo of Matthew 23:27, where Christ chastises the world's Tartuffes through a notable simile: "Woe unto you, scribes and Pharisees, hypocrites! for ye are like unto whited sepulchers, which indeed appear beautiful outward, but are within full of dead men's bones, and of all uncleanness." This is the sixth of Christ's seven woes against impostures, and the one most relevant to Tristram's undecorated, dappled, piebald marble: Tristram's sepulcher, and Sterne's. In the same way that Shakespeare literalizes on stage Yorick's *memento mori*, Sterne literalizes his and Tristram's tome as a marbled tomb, thus making *The Life and Opinions* the world's longest epitaph. That "tome" and "tomb" are homonyms in early modern

England simply intensifies the spectacular visual pun of the marble, which functions as part of Tristram's larger tomb motif, from "the tomb stone of Lucian" to the "*tomb of the lovers*," and all the haunted graveyards and "alas, poor *Yorick*s" in between.[58]

"To what end are such great tomes," asks Robert Burton in *The Anatomy of Melancholy*?[59] Sterne poses the same question and implies a modest answer via the marble's raw presentation. He knew that he—like all of humanity—was full of uncleanness, what the Calvinists call "absolute depravity," and others, "original sin," the inheritance of grief going all the way back to Eden. But rather than masking the human condition, as he believed that critics of volumes 1 and 2 would have preferred, Sterne faces it, providing a Momus window through which we might view "the soul stark naked," or at least more naked than most souls we view.[60] Such naked honesty, however, makes impossible for himself the kind of saccharine epitaph that Pope satirizes in the *Dunciad*, "the Sepulchral lies, our holy walls to grace"; or that Matthew Prior earlier satirized with Bishop Matthew Parker in mind, a man who took great care while alive to see that all aspects of his grave were properly managed:

> Then take Matt's word for it, the sculptor is paid,
>   That the figure is fine pray believe your own eye,
> Yet credit but lightly what more may be said,
>   For we flatter ourselves and teach marble to lie.[61]

Critics will say what they will about Sterne's autobiographical bawdry in the satires, and his sentimental and not-so-sentimental romances, but at least this much is clear: he does not hide behind a whited sepulcher. He does not teach his marble to lie, and thus refuses the Devil's perennial advice to write a white-washed tome of "what passes in a man's own mind."[62]

A similar honesty-in-light-of-spiritual-warfare theme accompanies the blank page, though critics have focused elsewhere. Peter de

Voogd summarizes the most persistent line of inquiry, describing the blankness as "witness to the impossibility of perfect communication in language," but that can be said of almost any word or image.[63] In a more whimsical direction, Elizabeth Harries calls the emptiness "aesthetic foolery," an extreme instance of the *non finito*, which it might very well be, but there is more to the story, as we find ourselves confronted by the Widow Wadman dilemma: to draw or not to draw the lady to our own specifications.[64] For a broader perspective on this type of dilemma, perhaps we do well first to consult Hartmann Schedel's *Nurnberg Chronicle* (1493), which also carries rhetorically blank pages—as aptly described by C.A. Patrides:

> The Nurnberger Chronik follows the traditional pattern, commencing with the creation and dividing history into Six Ages. There follows a description of the Last Judgment with appropriately terrifying illustrations ingeniously introduced by six folio pages left totally blank. This very blankness constitutes an obvious invitation to readers to take inventory of their lives before the horrid end.[65]

Sterne's blank page functions in almost exactly the same way, inviting us to take a moral inventory of our mental lives. It does so, however, with mischievous mirth. Patrides's "horrid end" mutes precisely that type of cosmic laughter invoked by Sterne's dark wit. And the standard by which we are to take this inventory is part of the black comedy: "Sit down, Sir, paint her to your own mind—as like your mistress as you can—as unlike your wife as your conscience will let you."[66] Tristram proposes "conscience" as the yardstick, which should immediately cause disquiet, given Yorick's insightful sermon on the subject and Tristram's earlier remark—pointed with a manicule—about the dangers of carrying around personal measuring sticks: "A dwarf who brings a standard along with him to measure his own size—take my word, is a dwarf in more articles than one," a bawdy remark and, simultaneously, an impeachment of pride.[67] And if this standard does not prove troubling enough, Sterne alludes to a second yardstick by which we might also take inventory, Matthew 5:27-28, where Christ memorably redefines adultery: "Ye have heard that it was said by them of old time, Thou shalt not commit adultery: But I say unto you, That whosoever looketh on a woman to lust after her hath committed adultery with her already in his heart." Seldom do we find this verse presented in a comic context, but Sterne's literary universe functions by an unexpected set of rules. Tolstoy's does not. He fretted over Christ's redefinition of adultery, used it as the epigraph for *The Kreutzer Sonata*, and argued for celibacy.[68] No one would accuse Tolstoy of taking Scripture lightly; perhaps he took it too seriously.

Sterne reaches no such drastic conclusion, that is, celibacy, but provides in his sermons more insight into the blank page's moral dilemma. In "The House of Feasting and the House of Mourning," for example, we hear that "in those loose and unguarded moments the imagination is not always at command," and thus "will forcibly carry [us] sometimes" where we would not go, much "like the unclean spirit" in Mark 9 took the child and "cast him into the fire to destroy him."[69] That is, the demonic imagination takes on a life of its own and oftentimes proves difficult to stop, until we find ourselves in the woods with demon lovers. Sterne provides another and related example in the apocalyptic "Description of the World" sermon. After referring to 2 Peter 3:10 and 1 Thessalonians 5:2, the thief-in-the-night verses, he remarks, "we are standing upon the edge of a precipice, with nothing but the single thread of human life to hold us up;—and [if] we fall unprepared in this thoughtless state, we are lost, and must perish for evermore."[70] In brief, Sterne implores us to be mindful of how we arrange our mental lives, which is precisely the blank page's sermonic message as well. Or, as Sterne puts it in his sermon on pride, and not without irony, "the most acceptable sacrifice we can offer [God] is a virtuous and upright mind."[71]

Conclusion

Dante said that the most sensitive readers of *The Divine Comedy* were those who regularly read the Bible and the Church Fathers. I believe him, insofar as authors can be trusted to say anything intelligent about how to read their works. The same might be said for *Tristram Shandy*, if by "sensitive readers" we mean those who detect the priestly garb underneath Sterne's piebald coat. And we may need to replace "Church Fathers" with Shakespeare and the Renaissance satirists. Six of one, half a dozen of the other. In his *Notes on the Sermons*, New provocatively addresses this topic of how to read Sterne's fiction in light of, or in spite of, his theology:

> Clearly, [Sterne] might have written *Tristram Shandy* without thinking very much about his Christian beliefs; as suggested, one fundamental insight of his religion is that people rarely live by their faith. Still, it might behoove readers of *Tristram* and *A Sentimental Journey* to entertain, at least for one moment, the possibility that the author of these fictions did not consistently hold beliefs that the author of the sermons would consider heretical, damnable, and quite simply wrong. In that moment of vacillation and oscillation, our own and Sterne's, we might discover an entirely different fiction from the one we thought we were reading.[72]

The second suggestion certainly rings true, that Sterne wrote as a self-aware Christian who made self-aware Christian arguments, if only readers would let them be. The first suggestion, however, the idea that Sterne might have ignored his Christianity, is all the more ironical now, given the Shandyverse's preoccupation with demonry. Indeed, there is such a thing as stating the obvious and, in corollary fashion, denying the obvious. We find ourselves in the awkward position of denying the obvious if we attempt to explain Sterne's satirical aims without recourse to the paranormal. That Sterne might have neglected this or that religious doctrine is a fair point, and likely true, but he plainly did not neglect the world of spiritual intrigue, as is evidenced most conspicuously by Tristram's avalanche of references to it. Absent the occult, in other words, we are hard-pressed to speak cogently about Sterne's comic sensibility.

The devils believe in *Tristram Shandy*'s critics, even if the critics do not believe in them. Most, it seems, do not. More to the present point, Sterne believed in paranormal realities and wrote a satire accordingly, setting Christian grace against the demonic in all its guises, but especially the all-too-sober pretense that comes from self-righteousness. *Tristram Shandy* is a counterstatement to Hell's gravity. It is an answer to Hell's rhetoric. Here, by the Shandean rite of exorcism, Sterne laughs away the foul fiends, those proud spirits who cannot endure to be mocked, and he invites us to do the same, if we should likewise want our demons gone.

3

Are the Sermons Funny?

The Victorian-era critic Percy Fitzgerald discovered in Sterne's sermons "much latent humor" and "a profound Rabelais[ian] twinkle." He lauded, in particular, the "Shandean handling" of "Elijah and the widow of Zarephath," by which he meant to imply that Sterne meant to imply that Elijah and the widow had great sex.[1] Sterne's contemporary Thomas Gray also found drollery in the sermons: "They are in the style I think most proper for the Pulpit, & shew a very strong imagination & a sensible heart: but you see him often tottering on the verge of laughter, & ready to throw his periwig in the face of the audience."[2] Exactly where the tottering occurs we do not know, but Gray obviously perceived a Comus-like spirit in Sterne's priesthood, and approved of it. So too have other readers.

On the contrary, critics have challenged the Sterne-as-Shandean-preacher thesis, none more effectively than Melvyn New. In the *Notes*, for example, New describes the sermons as decidedly not funny: "There is what might be called an opening jest in only six of the forty-five surviving sermons; in no sermon is there anything that can legitimately be called humor after the second paragraph."[3] A broader conclusion about Sterne's ecclesiastical sobriety follows: "The popular conception of the Shandean author is highly dubious. Sterne is not a jester in the pulpit, nor is he a secularist or shaftsburian, nor even a rhetorician, if by that label we mean (as John Traugott clearly does) someone who is preaching as a nominalist. What he is, dull as it might seem, is an Anglican clergyman."[4] W.B. Gerard amplifies the point, characterizing the sermons as "somber sacramental texts" caught up "in a Shandean whirlwind of paradox that mingled disorder with order, mischief with solemnity, and profitability with spirituality."[5] For Gerard, the comedy arrives not in the sermons themselves, but rather in the bizarre context surrounding their publication alongside—or perhaps astride—the bawdy half of Sterne's genius, *Tristram Shandy* and *A Sentimental Journey*. That most of the sermons were published under the banner of Yorick, partly for economic purposes, simply adds to the absurdist theater adjoining them, but—as the anti-Shandeans rightly suggest—such theater need say very little about the texts themselves.

We discover, then, competing views of the sermons' comic content. Some readers find humor in them, while others do not. Wherein lies the truth? Yorick reminds us in *A Sentimental Journey* that "there is nothing unmixt in this world," which is a good axiom in relation to Sterne's sermons and the question of comedy.[6] They are mixed. Set in their original theological and historical context, constrained by that context, the sermons are for the most part serious documents, yet not entirely so. For instance, I have identified several funny episodes beyond the opening jests, after which the modern critics discern only solemn preaching. Moreover, we must distinguish between the sermons themselves and the concomitant role they play as straight man, or counterpoint, in Sterne's oeuvre. That is, the sermons function as the predominantly sober half of a comic duo, and in their prevailing seriousness they become outrageously funny in a certain sense precisely because of their dialectical relationship to the fiction. Similarly, Abbott, in the Who's-on-First routine, amuses audiences as a direct result of his earnestness in relation to Costello's antics. Most double acts, or comedy duos, function in this way, and the sermons as counterpoints to the satires are no different. Sterne knew this. Following *Tristram Shandy*'s success, he described the second installment of the sermons as such: "These [homilies] you must know are to keep up a kind of balance in my shandaic character."[7] And a precarious balance it was. Sterne's playfulness endeared him to the likes of David Hume and Baron d'Holbach but annoyed many in the theological establishment, who deemed his wit excessive and his commitment to the clergy suspect.[8] Such indictments by powerful theologians, however, did not impress Sterne. He simply went about his business, writing dirty satires and preaching the gospel.

Full-Fledged Humor

We examine first "The history of Jacob," where Sterne reflects on the patriarch's unhappy life, one full of difficulties and disappointments. Of most interest is the sermon's recounting of Jacob and Leah's wedding night, if it can be called that. Jacob, of course, expected Rachel to come to the tent. He had worked seven years for Laban in order that he might marry his younger daughter, but Laban sent the older daughter instead, carrying out a deception that resembled Jacob's own act of trickery with his father, Isaac—a point not lost upon Sterne:

> I know not whether 'tis of any use to take notice of this singularity in the patriarch's life, in regard to the wrong he received from Laban, which was the very wrong he had done before to his father Isaac, when the infirmities of old age had disabled him from distinguishing one child from another: *Art thou my very son Esau? And he said, I am.* 'Tis doubtful whether Leah's veracity was put to the same test.[9]

Sterne's quip about the testing of Leah's veracity produces humor through a kind of ribald understatement. After seven years, Jacob was in no mood to ask a lot of questions, or any questions, for that matter. Inquiries were not made, and thus the scene quite naturally borders upon the slapstick. We cannot help but imagine Jacob's hurried demeanor, groping in the dark for whom he thought was Rachel, much like Yorick groped in the dark at the end of *A Sentimental*

Journey, trapped in a small hotel room with the Piedmontese lady and her *fille de chambre*. Similar to Yorick again, only in reverse order, Jacob grabbed a woman and ejaculated "O my God!" The author of Genesis gives us the rest of the scene: "It came to pass that in the morning, behold, it was Leah."

And like many subjects in Sterne's comic purview, bawdry begets more bawdry here. By invoking the testing Leah's veracity in conjunction with Jacob's deception of Isaac, Sterne calls our attention to fur, which bears a family resemblance to the issue of noses in *Tristram Shandy*. Jacob, we should remember, put the skin of a baby goat on his hands in an effort to seem hairy, so that the blind and dying Isaac would mistake Jacob for Esau—the hairy brother—and give him Esau's rightful blessing: "Esau my brother is a hairy man, and I am a smooth man," explains Jacob.[10] The ruse worked. Isaac predictably tested Jacob's veracity by touching his hands, and he passed the test because he felt hairy to the touch, thus causing Isaac to bless him. Might not a similar though obviously awkward observation be made about Jacob's approach to Leah, who also passed the test—in a manner of speaking—because she felt hairy to the touch? In fact, this seems to be the only test she passed. Ironically, Jacob's Lockean association of ideas between hair and veracity did not serve him well in this case, which intensifies the passage's multilayered humor.

Nor did Sterne's own dubious association of ideas between hair and veracity serve him well, a fact also not lost on the mindful priest, and one that brings us finally to the sermon's autobiographical dimension. Sterne plays the role Jacob on such a reading; Elizabeth Lumley, his wife, is Leah, and Rachel stands in for various sentimental and not-so-sentimental romances: Catherine Fourmantel, Eliza Draper, widows, prostitutes. The last inexorably calls to mind the merkin, a decorative pubic wig worn by early modern doxies to entice patrons and, simultaneously, conceal diseases. Merkins are the perennial Tartuffes in the carnal underworld's accessory closet, or, in a theological phrasing that probably crossed the dream logic of Sterne's comic imagination, the whited sepulchers in Matthew 23:27, "which indeed appear beautiful outward, but are within full of dead men's bones, and of all uncleanness." That Sterne saw merkins in his philandering is almost certain, and more obvious still is the resultant cognitive dissonance: "I do not know what is the matter with me," Sterne expostulates in a candid letter to his friend John Hall-Stevenson, "but I am sick and tired of my wife more than ever—and I am possessed by a Devil who drives me to town."[11] This is not the remark of a careless libertine, incidentally, nor is it the comment of a deist, given the Devil's conspicuous involvement as chauffer, though some critics have described Sterne in such terms. But, to the point at hand: we do not imagine Sterne testing the veracity of prostitutes wearing merkins, and therein we discover an obscure layer of self-deprecating humor in the sermon's amusing quip about Leah's veracity.[12]

Another funny episode appears in the "Abuse of Conscience" sermon, where Sterne makes an oblique reference to masturbation: "The conscience of a man, by long habits of sin, might (as the Scripture assures us, it may) insensibly become hard; and, like some tender parts of his body, by much stress, and continual hard usage, lose, by degrees, that nice sense and perception with which GOD and nature endowed it."[13] Such a veiled allusion need not be funny, and there is some question as to the degree of amusement here, but the passage gets funnier—I believe—as Sterne broadens the observation: "Did this never happen:—or was it certain that self-love could never hang the least bias upon the judgment:—or that the little interests below could rise up and perplex the faculties of our upper regions, and encompass them about with clouds and thick darkness."[14] The rhetorical technique is *erostesis*, one of Sterne's favorites, where a strong affirmation of the contrary is implied under the form of an earnest interrogation. In this case, Sterne indirectly observes that people often think below the belt, not above it, a sound remark if ever one existed. The idea is a staple in the history of comedy, from the lustful women in Aristophanes's *Lysistrata*, who find flimsy excuses to break ranks and see their husbands, to the parade of leading literary men who are motivated more by the id than the ego, including Sterne's sentimental reinvention of the Don Juan mythos, parson Yorick—a pinnacle of the archetype. "Little interests below" have been clouding rationality since Adam and Eve put on breeches, and we have no reason to believe that tomorrow will be any different. What we discover in the sermon on conscience, therefore, is an amusing and bawdy witticism, a brief passage about sexual motives set against the backdrop of a much larger comedy of moral sentiments (i.e., Sterne's experimental literary project). At the crux of said project, to use Arthur Cash's phrasing, is a "fundamental comic fact—that the heart can and does trick the head."[15] The fideist Blaise Pascal makes the same observation more famously: "The heart has its reasons of which reason knows nothing."[16] Sterne agrees, expressing just this insight in the sermon, but he also quickly supplements it with a mischievous sidebar: the heart is not the only piece of anatomy that tricks the head.

While we are on the topic of conscience, we might also notice that Sterne in the sermon makes clever use of Elijah's jest from 1 Kings 18:27.[17] The biblical episode in question involves a confrontation between Elijah and the priests of Baal, both of whom invoke their Gods. Baal's devotees perform their rituals first, yet Baal remains conspicuously absent, at which point Elijah lampoons them: "And it came to pass at noon that Elijah mocked them and said, cry aloud: for he is a god; either he is talking, or he is pursuing, or he is in a journey, or peradventure he sleepeth, and must be awaked." Other translations have Elijah suggesting that Baal might be on the toilet, a rendering softened by the King James Version. Regardless, the concept is clear: Baal cannot be found, just like the conscience cannot be found during various episodes of sinning and self-deception, an entertaining parallel noticed by Sterne:

Alas! Conscience had something else to do all this time than break in upon him: as Elijah reproached the god Baal, this domestic God was either talking, or pursuing, or was in a journey, or, peradventure, he slept and could not be awoke. Perhaps he was gone out in company, with HONOUR, to fight a duel;—to pay off some debt at play;—or dirty annuity, the bargain of his lust.—Perhaps, conscience all this time was engaged at home, talking aloud against petty larceny, and executing vengeance upon some such puny crimes as his fortune and rank, in life, secured him against all temptation of committing:—so that he lives as merrily,—sleeps as soundly in his bed;—and, at the last, meets death with as much unconcern,—perhaps, much more so than a much better man.[18]

Sterne takes what is already a witty taunt from the Old Testament and reformulates it to serve his purpose, which in this case is to puncture arrogant hypocrisy, mocking those who have too much confidence in the faculty of conscience. Such keen satire usually brings smiles to faces, unless we suddenly recognize ourselves as the targets of the ridicule, at which point we must choose either to laugh at our own shortcomings or fold our arms defensively, declaring Sterne to have gone too far at the expense of others.

Consider, too, the sermon "On humility," where comedy plays an interesting role. Here, Sterne burlesques the "false pretenses" of self-appointed popes and other tubsters who are quick to claim an astonishingly detailed knowledge of God's mind. He exempts the Quakers, a "harmless quiet people," but not the culture of revelatory hubbub from where they gleaned their "inner light" and other collateral tenets. The target is contemporary English enthusiasm writ large, in all of its grandiloquence, much of which Sterne traces back to "the religious cant of the last century":

When the *in-comings*, *in-dwellings*, and *out-lettings* of the Spirit were the subjects of so much edification; and, when as they do now, the most illiterate mechanicks, who as a witty divine said of them, were much fitter to *make* a pulpit, than to get into one,—were yet able so to frame their nonsense to the nonsense of the times, as to beget an opinion in their followers, not only that they pray'd and preach'd by inspiration, but that the most common actions of their lives were set about in the Spirit of the LORD.[19]

The "most common actions" presumably include eating, sleeping, and answering the call of nature, the last of which prompts us to imagine the evangelical street preacher's doctrine on inspired pooping. This is Rabelaisian playfulness. The more explicit amusement, however, arrives in the quip about pulpits, which Sterne borrows from "a witty divine"—very likely the Anglican priest Robert South. In a sermon titled "The Christian Pentecost," South proclaims, "None were thought fit for the Ministry but Tradesmen, and Mechanicks, because none else were allowed to have the Spirit. Those only were accounted like St. Paul who could work with their hands, and in a literal sense drive the Nail home, and be able to make a Pulpit before they preached in it."[20] This build-your-own-pulpit remark is a good example of an amusing jest because of the knowing slapstick it projects. We envision a fanatical minister—shoe hammer in hand—trying to preach without the benefit of theological awareness or cultural literacy. And so we detect a tragicomical disaster on the horizon, much like the disaster we foresee when Dr. Slop unsheathes the innovative forceps, a novelty that mangles rather than improves the human condition. Tristram's nose is evidence enough. Might we not say that Sterne, using the pulpit joke, makes an almost identical argument against novel theologies, often preached from itinerant stages built by the very innovators themselves? In both cases, forceps wielded by men out of their depth and pulpits made by tubsters, we raise our eyebrows and rightly assume the worst case. Contained within our imaginative assumption is a moment of comic relief, I think, one best illustrated by the seemingly inevitable asking of a time-tested rhetorical question: What could possibly go wrong?

Nor should the allusion to Swift's "Digression on Madness" go unnoticed. When Sterne recounts the "in-comings, in-dwellings, and out-lettings of the Spirit," we cannot help but hear an echo of the *Tale*'s crackpot scribbler explaining vapors and inspiration with his trademark pseudo-casuistic logic. In the *Notes*, New confirms this Swiftian echo.[21] Not that most of Sterne's parishioners made the connection, and nor perhaps did many of his subsequent readers. But those who do catch a glimpse of the manic tubster are happy to see him there, building his stage, advertising soon-to-be-published classics (e.g., *A General History of Ears, A Critical Essay upon the Art of Canting*), and calling out to his "worthy brethren" in "Moorfields," a place known for traveling medicine shows and the Bedlam insane asylum.[22] There is no substitute for good references. Sterne's allusion to Swift obviously does not constitute a joke proper, but it nonetheless amuses in a strategically designed way. It provides comic ambience, nicely interrupting the idea of a purely somber sacramental text.

Half-Fledged Humor

In addition to straightforward comedy, or mostly straightforward comedy, the sermons also contain half-humorous episodes, which leave us uncertain about the extent to which we should laugh. Sterne scatters fragments of mirth, similar in a structural sense to the half-swear words shared between Margarita and the abbess of Andoüillets.[23] We are left, then, to supply the unstated parts and—in a very real sense—to complete the humor ourselves. In rhetorical terms, this is called an enthymeme. In aesthetics, the *non-finito*. And in a Shandean vocabulary, we are talking about such things as the structure of *A Sentimental Journey*'s conclusion, Walter's half-finished speech on duration in volume 3, and the blank page's persistent allure (i.e., the Widow Wadman dilemma), where we are to complete the portrait ourselves: "Paint her to your own mind."[24] Whether in the satires or the sermons, Sterne often amicably halves the matter, leaving us to flesh out various scenarios in our own imaginations.[25]

Examples will illustrate the idea. In "The Levite and his concubine," Sterne invites us to poeticize the sour faces of those grave parishioners who hear the word "concubine." Some listeners, of course, might remember that the concubine, her father, and the Levite were "a most sentimental group."[26] Others will not, however, as Sterne very well knew: "Give but the outlines of a story,—let *spleen* or *prudery* snatch the pencil, and they will finish it with so many hard strokes, and with so dirty a colouring, that candour and courtesy will sit in torture as they look at it."[27] Of particular interest, here, is the reference to "dirty colouring." It causes us to wonder about what goes through the minds of the church's moral busybodies, especially when they think about concubines. Do they envision a gentle couple holding hands? Doubtful. How about naked women, or men, in compromising positions? Almost certainly, and with such speculation there is humor. In other words, the real comedy in Sterne's spleen-and-prudery remark lies off stage, not in the thoughts of those who overstatedly recoil at the hint that someone transgressed a prudish law of decency, but rather in the minds of those who contrast Sterne's cheerfulness against the puritan's bothered, gloomy affect. "Puritanism: The haunting fear that someone, somewhere, may be happy," as H.L. Mencken declared.[28] And while Sterne is certainly not acerbic like Mencken, he shares with all existential philosophers an ironic attitude toward morality mongering, especially of the religious type. But grave temperaments seldom respond to direct critique, and so Sterne provides instead merry indirection as a powerful corrective, a "solvent for the removal of dangerous delusions."[29] If we play along with Sterne and imagine what he implies to be the grave congregants' semi-pornographic daydreams, then we discover in the "Levite and his concubine" a moment of impish mirth, which is probably why

William Rose, Sterne's thoughtful contemporary and anthologizer, warned that the sermon "wears too gay an aspect."[30]

The comic *non-finito* is more elusive in the case of "Elijah and the widow of Zarephath." Given Fitzgerald's vague positing of a Rabelaisian twinkle in the text, we cannot help but search for remote sexual connotations, unexpected double entendres, and the like. At the same time, this is a charity sermon. The occasion drives the purpose, and the sermon's dramatic pathos functions primarily to encourage acts of kindness toward the poor, not to intimate clandestine romance. Moreover, on the question of sex, perhaps the sermon is neither clandestine nor Shandean in its arrangement. Maybe the sex is fairly obvious, or hidden in plain sight. Why would we not speculate in a commonsensical way about the relationship between Elijah and the widow, one that proves natural to the sentiments of tender hearts who have found each other in an extremely stressful situation? Why might they not form an amorous connection, and why—just as easily—might not the author of 1 Kings simply pass over the details in silence, out of some measure of modesty or priority?[31] Indeed, Saint Paraleipomenon may require it. If there is something mischievous at work in the sermon, or righteously impolite, then it is not Sterne's dramatization of the story, but rather the verse he quotes on behalf of Elijah. Of course, the verse we most expect to see in this context is James 1:27, the nearly always-invoked passage on matters of widows and children: "Pure religion and undefiled before God and the Father is this, to visit the fatherless and widows in their affliction, and to keep himself unspotted from the world."[32] But Sterne conspicuously avoids this standard piece of Scripture, preferring instead Ecclesiasticus 4:10: "Be as a father unto the fatherless, and instead of an husband unto their mother." To be sure, James and Ecclesiasticus make similar points, but the latter is the bawdier option, or—at minimum—the option more easily used for a bawdy implication. What might it mean to stand in for the husband? What exactly does the metonym entail? Sterne more than likely wondered the same and so presumably chose Ecclesiasticus because of its ambiguous, potentially suggestive, potentially indecorous connotation. Therein is the comedy, or what might be deemed the Rabelaisian twinkle.

Other half-funny episodes come to mind, more than can be noted here. Why, for example, does Sterne mention the gods' "wives and mistresses" in the "Advantages of Christianity to the world," if not to provide some wry commentary on the history of marital strife?[33] Or recall—in "The Prodigal Son"—the half-formed character sketch of the heavily weathered *valet de chamber*, who bears a striking resemblance to Gussie Finknottle from the P.G. Wodehouse sagas: "Many an experienced undertaker would have been deceived by his appearance and started embalming on sight."[34] The beleaguered valet, Sterne explains, has "thrice made *the tour of Europe with success*," that is, "without breaking his own or his Pupil's neck," a witty epexegesis that nicely undercuts the Grand Tour's humbug rhetoric, which is the sermonic aim.[35] We complete the half-formed satirical scene in our own ways, complaining about pretentious travel, travelers, and those who market said traveling, perhaps remembering Tristram's dance with Nanette in the process.[36]

Or, as one last example of the comic *non-finito*, we discover Sterne's sarcastic remark in "The parable of the rich man and Lazarus": "all discourses of religion and virtue" in Christendom, he notes, probably appear to the outsider as "matters of speculation," because Christians "seem to be agreed in no one thing, but speaking well—and acting ill."[37] The sentiment is too general to be fully comical but specific enough to be partway funny. As such, it cajoles us into finishing the humor. Maybe Swift's Lilliputians help, those factions embroiled in a doctrinal dispute over which end of the egg is to be preferred. The Big-Endians. The Little-Endians. Or perhaps we invoke Ambrose Bierce's bitingly ironic definitions in *The Devil's Dictionary*, which are like little mirrors held up to the grave Mrs. Grundys of the world: Christian, "One who believes that the New Testament is a divinely inspired book admirably suited to the spiritual needs of his neighbor." Heaven, "A place where the wicked cease from troubling you with talk of their personal affairs, and the good listen with attention while you expound your own."[38] Sterne's comic hints and innuendos come to full life with our aid, and I do not think he would have it otherwise.

Sterne suggests in a letter that "The true feeler always brings half of the entertainment along with him," which is another way of saying that he expects readers to be active, whether responding to full-fledged or half-fledged comedy.[39] He imagines an audience capable of surmising and inferring. Indeed, he requires it, as Tristram also usefully explains:

> Writing, when properly managed (as you may be sure I think mine is), is but a different name for conversation. As no one who knows what he is about in good company would venture to talk all;—so no author who understands the just boundaries of decorum and good-breeding would presume to think all: The truest respect which you can pay to the reader's understanding is to halve this matter amicably, and leave him something to imagine, in his turn, as well as yourself.[40]

Might not the same be said also of Yorick's sermonic conversations, with the appropriate theological caveats? That is, Sterne fulfills his calling as a priest by teaching religious truths and administering the sacraments, but even in this work the value of real participation should be stressed. Arguably, in fact, the value is all the more important. What is religion, if not participatory? What is "a flap upon the heart," to use Sterne's description of genuine sermonizing, if the heart is not in pilgrimage?[41] Both the satires and the sermons should therefore be understood as robustly collaborative in their deep structures. They are interchanges that await completion, writings that leave room for us to maneuver, to breathe, and—no doubt—to fall seven times a day.[42] Sterne, perhaps more so than any author, calls on us to be self-deprecatingly realistic about our own rogue imaginations.

The Comedies of Publication and Plagiarism

We arrive, now, at the comedy of Sterne's plagiarism and the stir caused by the publication of his sermons alongside the satires and with Yorick as a pseudonym. Both make the sermons funnier, but in different ways. The circumstances of publication strike many of us as inherently amusing, even farcical, and the extent to which we imagine these circumstances is the extent to which we experience a heightened sense of delight. Not that our feelings of delight fall squarely on the sermons; rather, we appreciate the sermons in all of their Anglican good sense, piety, and pathos, but we simultaneously realize that their predominant straightness produces a comic atmosphere insofar as the straightness amplifies the bawdry.[43] This is Sterne's genius, to publish sermons that function in a dual manner, effectively preaching the gospel and concurrently intensifying the comic value of the satires, replete with indelicate jokes and half-naked comedies of error. In this way, the sermonic volumes are part and parcel of the Shandean whirlwind, not Shandean in content but rather Shandean by virtue of how they appeared on the scene, printed as well, incidentally, in the same small octavo format as *Tristram Shandy*, an obvious departure from the typical format of eighteenth-century sermon collections.[44] Even Sterne's layout had comical import.

All of this adds up to mirth, and more mirth still if we follow Ben Franklin's example and quip about Sterne's mischievousness: "[Since] they cannot yet afford to maintain both a Clergyman and a Dancing-master," he observed of the impoverished Fort Pitt, "the Dancingmaster reads Prayers and one of Tristram Shandy's Sermons every Sunday."[45] But not everyone played along with Sterne's comedy of publication, including the bothered critic Owen Ruffhead, a Sterne contemporary who admired the sermons' sober content but not the means by which they first saw print: "We think it becomes us to make some animadversions on the manner of their publication, which we consider as the greatest outrage against Sense and Decency that has been offered since the first establishment of Christianity—an outrage that scarce would have been tolerated even in the days of paganism."[46] Ruffhead was not alone in his opinion, but his expression of outrage is nonetheless noteworthy, and, from an alternative point of view, humorous. In fact, the more vehemently such outrage is expressed, the funnier it becomes from the Shandean perspective, which is to say that the Ruffheads of the world unwittingly added to Sterne's comic project by virtue of their grim-faced overreactions. Sterne knew this, of course, and appreciated how these grave critics further vindicated his wit.

Concerning Sterne's comedy of plagiarism, the important point to highlight is that Sterne did what every other eighteenth-century priest did, and this was to borrow content from the theological writings and sermons of others. Such behavior was a mark of commonsense and—at times—a matter of survival, as Sterne knowingly demonstrates in the *Rabelaisian Fragment*. Here, the desperate Homenas—scheduled to give a homily the next morning—asks a perfectly sound rhetorical question: "Why, may not a Man lawfully call in for Help, in this, as well as any other human emergency?" And thus he goes to his books:

> So without any more Argumentation, except starting up and nimming down from the Top Shelf but one, the second Volume of Clark tho' without any felonious Intension in so doing, He had begun to clap me in (making a Joynt first) Five whole Pages, nine round Paragraphs, and a Dozen and a half of good Thoughts all of a Row; and because there was a confounded high Gallery,— was transcribing it away, Like a little black Devil. Now—quoth *Homenas* to Himself, "Tho' I hold all this to be fair and square Yet, if I am found out, there will be the Deuce & all to pay".[47]

In wonderfully caricatured form, Homenas reflects typical clerical behavior. And Sterne, too, behaved typically when faced with looming Sunday deadlines, finding inspiration (and more) in a variety of sources, oftentimes imaginatively reworking the borrowed passages in the process, as James Gow has recently demonstrated.[48]

What remains decidedly atypical and more dubious, however, is the way Sterne framed the robberies in the preface to his first collection of printed sermons, feigning forgetfulness about the sheer amount of material he imported and the means by which he kept track of it. Or not:

> I have nothing to add but that the reader, upon old and beaten subjects, must not look for many new thoughts,—'tis well if he has new language; in three or four passages, where he has neither one nor the other, I have quoted the author I made free with—there are some other passages where I suspect I may have taken the same liberty,—but 'tis only suspicion, for I do not remember it is so, otherwise I should have restored them to their proper owners.[49]

Kraft offers the funniest commentary I have seen on this passage by suggesting that "to refresh his memory would have taken too long."[50] Sterne apologizes "rather lamely"—New observes—for what is obviously a breach of etiquette.[51] There was no expectation of citing sources for sermons delivered to a live congregation, but printed sermons were another matter. Normal practice was to give credit. Sterne knew this, but he also knew what every serious writer has always known: good writers pilfer. "Immature poets imitate; mature poets steal," as T.S. Eliot said, or, to use Robert Burton's phrasing, "our poets steal from Homer," and "our story-dressers do as much."[52] Not that Sterne's guilt should be excused. Not that he excused himself. There is something delightfully confessional and autobiographical in the note we discover scribbled on the first leaf of one of Yorick's sermons: "For this sermon I shall be hanged,—for I have stolen the greater part it. Doctor Paidagunes found me out. ☞ Set a thief to catch a thief."[53] With the reference to "Paidagunes," or the Pedagogue, in particular, Sterne prophetically signals to his readers that he anticipates the charge of larceny, and that he accepts it, with one crucial caveat: scholars should not behave self-righteously as they uncover his borrowings: "set a thief to catch a thief" to be sure.

Sterne clearly imagined a future wherein scholars discovered more of his pilfering. Such discoveries, he furthermore understood, would intensify the irony of his feigned forgetfulness about his rhetorical theft. And it has. Upon every new discovery of an uncited source in the sermons, Sterne's convenient amnesia proves more amusing. Thus, on the question of plagiarism, we might say that Sterne's sermons have gotten funnier over time, as more borrowings have come to light. Lansing Hammond's meticulous work in *Laurence Sterne's Sermons of Mr. Yorick* (1948), for example, produced a new round of comedy precisely because we began to appreciate even more fully Sterne's larceny.[54] With New's *Notes*, a second wave of comic pleasure arrived, as the borrowings began to look like the chocolates on that treadmill in the iconic scene from *I Love Lucy*, where Lucy and Ethel try to keep pace with the candy factory's assembly line, only to be overwhelmed eventually by little bonbons. Sterne's pilfering produces a similar comedy of scale, bringing us ultimately, perhaps inevitably, to New's memorable warning: "It would be foolhardy to provide a percentage figure for borrowed material, but this I can suggest: one risks one's reputation by pointing to any passage in any sermon and insisting on hearing Sterne's unique voice, for tomorrow we may discover, in the vast sea of sermon literature available to him, the particular drop he swallowed."[55]

Conclusion

There is an old witticism about a man who claimed it was easy to stop drinking. He knew this because he had done it a thousand times. Perhaps in the same way it was easy for Sterne to stop quipping. Yet he was not a harlequin in the pulpit. Far from it. The sermons are earnest in the way we expect eighteenth-century Anglican sermons to be earnest, and the humor is relatively scarce and appropriate, or appropriately inappropriate, as the case might be. In either case, the humor is there, reinforcing what one of the sermons' early reviewers so rightly observed: Sterne is "no gloomy religionist," to the consternation of gloomy religionists everywhere.[56] The sermons amuse, at least in certain ways, at least in places. Some passages are funnier than others, some bawdier than expected, and all indicative of a priest who found the comical in otherwise serious and often melancholic circumstances. If a parson is to err on the side of risqué mirth or forbidding severity, then let risqué mirth always be the problem. And for those who affect severe postures at the thought of Sterne's playfulness with the word "concubine," and for those who dislike the idea of a priest telling jokes of the sort that impress fishermen and prostitutes, I recite an important question that C.S. Lewis once posed: "Who wants to hear a particular claret abused by a fanatical teetotaler?"

On the broader issue of why Sterne so dramatically blended the sacred and the profane, besides the economic motive, at least this much might be noticed: he printed the sermons alongside the bawdy satires so that the William Warburtons of the world would disapprovingly observe that the same author who wrote the former also wrote the latter, which is exactly what Warburton did. He fell for it, as the religiously grave have been doing ever since. Embedded in the fabric of Sterne's genius is a simple response to all such haughty charges of Christian impropriety: concessio. Paromologia. Giving no resistance, Sterne admits it. He presents himself as the man who thought copiously about God and sex, not necessarily always in that order and not always, or perhaps not even frequently, in a way that reassured his fellow Christians. This self-presentation on Sterne's part constitutes one of the great acts of spiritual maturity in the history of Christianity, and, I believe, is almost certainly why Thomas Jefferson described his works as "the best course on morality ever written."[57]

4

Maria in the Biblical Sense

Maria of Moulins appears twice in Sterne. Near the end of *Tristram Shandy*, she plays vespers on the flute and keeps company with a pet goat. We meet her again in *A Sentimental Journey*, because Yorick cannot resist "an impulse" to go and find her. She continues to roam the French countryside, flute in hand, but her goat has been replaced by a small dog named Sylvio. In both scenes, she is beautiful; in the second, "scarce earthly."[1] And perhaps it goes without saying that the Maria vignettes contain a sexual undercurrent, as we might expect, yet those contemporary critics who most disliked Sterne's bawdry discovered in the pieces something acceptable, if not sublime. Both, for example, were reprinted in *The Beauties of Sterne*, and the second—the more sentimental of the two—gave rise to an avalanche of illustrations and engravings, the most famous of which appeared on Joseph Wedgwood's tea services, a sign that Maria had been deemed safe for polite society's consumption.[2]

The Maria episodes remain relatively safe in certain modern lines of criticism. Most notably, Elizabeth Kraft gives Tristram and Yorick the benefit of the doubt, discovering in these men an earnest attempt to comfort a melancholic young woman, or to be comforted by her, as the case might be. Kraft admits to an eroticism in the scenes but remains dubious on claims of sexual intercourse: Maria "is quite vulnerable, but [Yorick] does not turn that vulnerability to his sexual advantage," Kraft determines, and nor does Tristram.[3] This is the innocent school of thought. On the contrary, others have read the Maria vignettes in a much bawdier register. Valerie Purton, for instance, speculates that Tristram's steps are "broken and irregular" not because he is overcome by grief but rather because he carries Maria back to the hotel room, which then cogently explains Tristram's final expostulation: "What an excellent inn at Moulins!"[4] Thomas Keymer detects a pronounced innuendo in all of the motions and emotions toward Maria, while Paul McGlynn sees more than an innuendo: Tristram proves "grossly deviant," while Yorick engages in "sentimental masturbation," "sadism," and "pornography," seemingly all at once.[5] Keeping a due distance from the Marquis de Sade school of thought, Melvyn New, W.G. Day, and John Dussinger identify an erotic religiosity in the Maria episodes; they confirm the bawdry but observe, too, a theological self-awareness that tempers any effort to find a pornographic leer, either in the characters themselves or in the author's intent.[6] Other critics have suggested much the same, locating the Maria scenes somewhere on a continuum between sentimentality and smut. Exactly where on the continuum remains a matter of conscience, but Sterne points in a general direction: Rabelais, Cervantes, a striking young woman, music, handkerchiefs, older men who struggle with sexual propriety, and an oblique reference to what the Americans call "the Brazilian." One of Sterne's best clues, however, has gone unnoticed, and this is an allusion to Tamar of Judah-and-Tamar fame. It is a key allusion, I believe, because Tamar's presence gives us a new set of premises from which to reason, and, consequently, a richer view of what takes place on the outskirts of Moulins.

My claim is that Sterne builds the Maria episodes in *Tristram Shandy* and *A Sentimental Journey* on Genesis 38. Here, we discover a sexual encounter between Judah and his daughter-in-law, Tamar, who disguised herself as a prostitute. That he did not recognize Tamar may seem far-fetched, but she concealed her face with a veil. A dark one, presumably. And we also know that Judah asked very few questions: he simply agreed to a payment plan involving a goat. Subsequently, Tamar got pregnant, embarrassed Judah, and became a matriarch in the line that produced David and, eventually, Jesus of Nazareth. Exactly why Maria should have something to do with the Tamar story, however, is by no means obvious, nor should we want it to be. This is a deeper riddle. The mysterious Maria stands in for Tamar, as Sterne cleverly constructs the allusion, while Tristram, Yorick, and the inquisitive reader play the role of Judah, or possibly Onan, depending. Granted, the Maria vignettes do not parallel the biblical account exactly. Rather, they function as a tragi-comical answer to Sterne's counterfactual inquiry: What would have happened to Tamar had she not become pregnant? One answer, Sterne's impish answer in *Tristram Shandy*, is that she would have received a pet goat by which to remember the ill-fated encounter. In broader terms, Tamar—I think Sterne speculates— would have become a wandering daughter, which is another way of describing a particular type of prostitute (e.g., Bunny Lebowski).[7] If the Tamar–Maria connection is sound, then there is no getting away from prostitution. This fact need not diminish the genuine pathos we detect in the Maria scenes, but it alters it. Had George Carter comprehended Sterne's allusion to Tamar, for example, he would not have posed his daughter in the attitude of Maria, we assume, and the duchess d'Orléans may not have posed herself likewise.[8] Informed by the Judah-and-Tamar connection, we encounter an unanticipated Maria, less docile and more cunning than before, a Maria who through ingenuity and grit makes the best out of a bad situation (i.e., the curate forbid her banns). And her motive is straightforward, at least in one respect. She wants to get pregnant, preferably by a man of means, and so proceeds accordingly, performing the-young-woman-in-trouble routine. The sentimentally minded men in the surrounding villages have no doubt tried to rescue her, especially the older men, and just as surely they have realized, often to their astonishment, how quickly delicacy becomes concupiscence.

A Brief Summary of Genesis 38

Because the Judah-and-Tamar story is obscure to most modern critics, a brief account of Genesis 38 will prove useful. Judah, one of Joseph's brothers, married the daughter of a Canaanite woman named Shua, and they had three sons: Er, Onan, and Shelah. Er married Tamar but was "wicked in the Lord's sight," and so "the Lord put him to death." At this point, Judah required Onan to perform his brotherly duty by having sex with Tamar in order to produce a legal heir for Er. Readers unacquainted with Levirate marriage practices may find this behavior odd, but it was normal at the time and later codified in Deuteronomy 25: 5-6:

> If brethren dwell together, and one of them die and have no child, the wife of the dead shall not marry without unto a stranger: her husband's brother shall go in unto her and take her to him to wife, and perform the duty of a husband's brother unto her. And it shall be that the firstborn which she beareth shall succeed in the name of his brother which is dead, that his name be not put out of Israel.

Onan had another idea in mind, as is evidenced by the word that now carries his name: onanism—made famous in England by the anonymously published bestseller *Onania* (1716). The term denotes *coitus interruptus* and more generally masturbation, central themes in Sterne's comic purview. Onan's conduct bothered God, who "slew him also," but not before Onan became known as the man without a sandal, an insult directed toward those who failed to perform this brotherly duty, wherein "sandal" functioned as a euphemism for the vagina.[9] Distraught, but nonetheless mindful of tradition, Judah then promised to Tamar his third son, Shelah, when he came of age, but Judah later reneged, perhaps fearing that Tamar was cursed. Thus, she remained a widow in her father's house. Judah's wife died soon after, at which point he traveled north with a friend to sheer sheep; along the way he met a harlot, or so he believed, sitting by the gates of a small town. They negotiated sex; Judah agreed to send her a kid, but the veiled harlot insisted upon having something in the meanwhile as collateral, and so Judah gave her his signet. When the baby goat was finally sent, Judah's man could not find the prostitute, and a few months later, Judah—home again—discovered that Tamar was pregnant, or "with child by whoredom," as the King James Bible puts it. He immediately demanded Tamar's public execution, at which point she, in one of the most instructive moments in all of biblical literature, revealed Judah's signet. The execution was abruptly cancelled.

The Bible does not condemn Tamar for what she did, nor does the rabbinical literature, a point worth stressing. In fact, the book of Ruth praises her in the form of a blessing placed on the house of Boaz: "And let thy house be like the house of Pharez, whom Tamar bare unto Judah."[10] More than coincidentally, too, the Ruth–Boaz romance involves a young woman who seduced an older man. This obviously parallels the Tamar and Judah account, minus the deception, though Ruth's approach to Boaz was certainly less than kosher (i.e., she showed up late at night and naked, after Boaz had been drinking). Highlighting the age difference, Boaz—in fact—twice refers to Ruth as his "daughter" before they are publicly married, in what can only be described from the modern perspective as an uncomfortable nomenclature.[11] And neither perhaps should it go unnoticed that Ruth came from the Moabites, a tribe whose origin can be traced back to the story of Lot and his two daughters.[12] The Tamar plot, in other words, is part of a larger theme in the Old Testament about young women, older men, and unexpected sex, a theme that undoubtedly interested Sterne.

And Sterne, of course, knew the stories well. In "The History of Jacob," for example, he refers to Judah's "adulterous" behavior, by which he means the illicit rendezvous with Tamar.[13] He alludes to Ruth and Lot elsewhere, but even without such direct references, we are right to assume that Sterne had a detailed knowledge of these scriptures. The

Bible was the primary tool of his trade. He preached the good news from it and clung to it in times of need. And when pressed about the source of his original style in *Tristram Shandy*, he replied, "the daily reading of the Old and New Testaments."[14] When scholars argue for allusions, biblical or otherwise, the first order of business is to show that the author in question knew the work at issue. This is often the most difficult task. For instance, when Thomas Keymer connects Yorick's Maria to Marvell's "Nymph complaining for the Death of Her Faun," he first has to demonstrate that Sterne knew Marvell's poetry, which requires arguments about Marvell's influence in mid-eighteenth-century England, Sterne's friendship with the Marvell enthusiast Thomas Hollis, and so on.[15] Keymer makes a convincing case, but the route is decidedly circuitous, and his arguments are based largely upon indirect evidence and reasonable speculation. No such elaborate effort is required for the allusion to Tamar. Because we presuppose Sterne's deep awareness of the biblical source material, the task at hand is a simpler one; we need only to explain how the evidence shows the Tamar allusion, which is more obvious than the Marvell allusion, I think, and more central to Sterne's purposes in the Maria scenes.

Tristram Shandy's Maria

Early in volume 9, Tristram declares that keyholes have inspired a lot of sinning. By "keyholes," he means both keyholes and keyholes, a double entendre borrowed from *The Song of Solomon*, which is to say that Sterne's penchant for bawdy euphemisms has a distinguished pedigree.[16] But is the "inn at Moulins" such a euphemism?[17] If so, then we have an opening to the scene's bawdy potential and, too, a framework wherein Tamar might be discovered.

As far as euphemisms for the vagina go, "inn" is not a particularly common one, but nor is it obscure. A prostitute in Thomas Dekker's

Northward Ho, for example, confesses, "I have bin an Inne for any guest."[18] In Thomas Killigrew's *Parsons Wedding* (1639), a lady of the evening observes similarly that some women are "Palaces," some "Hospitals," and some "Inns," an idea recycled in Robertson's "On a Lady of Pleasure" (1749).[19] Undoubtedly, Sterne would have known the euphemism. It existed alongside numerous others to which he had access: coin purses, gates, crevices, open secrets, old hats, little shoes, nothings, as in *Much Ado about Nothing*, button holes, slits in petticoats, the mother of all saints, the monosyllable, ellipses, and—in some cases—etcetera, to name a few. The "inn at Moulins" almost certainly functions in the same way, which explains—among other things—Ralph Griffiths's complaint against the apostrophe. Griffiths, a persistent critic of Sterne's bawdry, found the Maria scene laudable in its sentimentality, except for "the abrupt transition in the two last lines," which served "but to *spoil all*, by an ill-timed stroke of levity."[20] After chiding Sterne, Griffiths deletes the scene's conclusion before reprinting it in the *Monthly Review*.[21] William Holland, editor of *The Beauties of Sterne*, takes similar action, omitting the apostrophe in order to avoid an indecorous connotation, because an indecorous connotation is rather difficult to avoid otherwise.[22] Of course, we could declare Tristram's "inn at Moulins" an innocent entendre, much like the earl of Clonmell declared La Fleur's making "merry with his pipe" an "innocent entendre" in *A Sentimental Journey*.[23] The option is available, but given the striking tonal change in Tristram's hasty apostrophe, and given Sterne's penchant for hiding bawdry in plain sight, we are better served to assume that the dirty sense runs alongside the literal sense in this case. Also, on a side note and in point of fact, La Fleur did make "merry with his pipe" in more ways than one; the earl of Clonmell, no doubt well intentioned, was very likely mistaken about his discovery of an innocent entendre.

We have reason to pursue a less than innocent reading of the Maria episode, but this is to notice nothing, yet, of Tamar. Enter the goat. It is, Peter de Voogd notices, "an animal that somewhat distracts from the sentimental dignity of the scene."[24] Indeed, the goat punctures any hope of unadulterated sentimentality: after Maria looks "wistfully" and "alternately" for some time at Tristram and the beast, Tristram asks, "Well [...] what resemblance do you find?"[25] The goat also carries the disruptive connotations of Bacchus, Dionysius, dryads, and fauns, all of which reinforce the scene's fertility-ritual motif, causing us to recall that same motif in volume 7, where Tristram invokes "saint Booger" and dances with Nanette.[26] But if the goat is part of a goat–signet allusion to the Judah-and-Tamar story, then we need to discover a signet and, moreover, a rationale by which Maria came to possess the animal. The rationale comes first and requires from us a prescient imaginative leap: the man who gave her the goat, the Judah archetype—maybe a distinguished priest, or perhaps a well-known baron—did so in order to keep a promise; we assume this for the sake of the argument. When she received the goat and presumably some money, she promptly returned whatever signifying collateral she held, because she was not pregnant. In other words, the signet attached to the goat is gone by the time Tristram arrives, which makes proving its existence difficult. Had Maria become pregnant, then her saga would have ended differently. The signet would have shown paternity, and Maria, after negotiating an arrangement with the soon-to-be father, would have settled into motherhood. Instead, however, we find the goat.

If this backstory for Maria and her goat seems far-fetched, then I concede the point, until we read *A Sentimental Journey*. That is, we discover the full possibility of this backstory in the future, which seems in keeping with Sterne's nonlinear mode of storytelling.[27] Marked with an "S" in the corner, Tristram's handkerchief is the signifying item used to alert readers to the possibility of signets. When Yorick meets Maria, he inquires over "a pale thin person of a man, who had sat down betwixt her and her goat about two years before."[28] She remembers Tristram on two accounts: first, that "she saw the person pitied her," which is a euphemism, and second, that "her goat had stolen his handkerchief." She kept the token "ever since in her pocket to restore it to him in case she should ever see him again, which, she added, he had half promised her."[29] Exactly how the goat stole the handkerchief is uncertain, but one ordinarily notices such a thing. Perhaps Tristram was distracted, or maybe he put down his coat in pursuit of a zesty enterprise. Maybe both. Or maybe Maria blames the goat as a cover story, a red herring, because the real reason Tristram gave her the handkerchief might be a matter too delicate to recount in polite company; Genesis 38:9 is an exception in world literature that proves this general rule of propriety.[30] Regardless, Maria has the handkerchief in hand and Tristram's half promise, with the caveat that he appears to have kept the other half of the promise.

We might also, at this point, retrospectively determine that Maria's flute is a signet, though not as clearly marked as Tristram's and Yorick's handkerchiefs. We do not know from whom she received the flute, nor do we know how she learned to play it, but, in light of the new information gleaned from *A Sentimental Journey*, we can make an educated guess: La Fleur. He behaves in an unusual way when he meets Maria's mother, "pass[ing] the back of his hand twice across his eyes," and he regularly makes himself and others "merry with his pipe."[31] Given La Fleur's expertise with the flute and with the language of seduction, it is reasonable to surmise that he is a factor behind the curate's decision to forbid Maria's wedding. The curate himself is also a likely factor, while we are on the subject. When the postilion alludes to the "intrigue" surrounding the curate's decision, the attentive reader cannot help but implicate the curate as a less-than-objective witness at the very least, and—more than likely—an active participant.[32] That is, he probably had some form of sex with Maria, or she with him. In either case, the intrigue derailed Maria's wedding, placing her in a kind of limbo similar to that in-between state experienced by Tamar, who waited in vain to marry Shelah, Judah's third son. To be sure, Maria's details are not Tamar's details, but the general situation is remarkably similar: both women lose love, and both women wait for a new opportunity that, given their circumstances, will need to be unconventional in nature.

Once alerted to the possibility of a Tamar allusion, we also see other details in a new light. Take, for instance, Tristram's reference to those "Damsels in the gate-way," each of whom gives a "sisterly kiss," if paid appropriately.[33] Tristram's emphasis on the innocence of the kiss is itself suspicious and should prompt a question about what Sterne hides. The language is too insistently guiltless to be guiltless, in other words, but the clue—"sisterly"—is difficult to discern, until we find ourselves in Genesis 38 and Deuteronomy 25, where sisterly kisses function in a far less innocent sense, if by "innocent" we mean "nonsexual."[34] And neither should the bawdy import of "damsels" go unnoticed. By the time Sterne used the term, it had become quaint in many circles, not straightforwardly descriptive, though the King James Bible regularly uses it and so kept it in circulation. But of most interest to us is the metaphorical meaning of "damsel," as Ephraim Chambers observes in his *Cyclopedia*: "a kind of Utensil put in Beds to warm old Mens Feet withal."[35] More specifically, the "damsel" was a piece of hot iron placed in a metal cylinder, which worked as a primitive space heater, a substitute for the real thing. Spoken in this way, "damsel" playfully alludes to 1 Kings 1: 1-4, where an old and weakened David finds for himself a young and beautiful damsel to keep him warm at night: Abishag the Shunammite, a virgin.[36] The author of Kings is quick to stress that David "knew her not," but the biblical scene nonetheless raises more questions than it answers. Ultimately, what Sterne meant by "damsels in the gate-way" must remain indeterminate, of course, if Sterne's multilayered narrative is to flourish, but somewhere within the several meanings of "damsel" lurks this satirical meaning tied to 1 Kings, and that Sterne could resist such a meaning seems unlikely. Or, put differently, Sterne uses these damsels and their sisterly kisses to provoke the attentive reader's search for sexual intrigue, all the while giving the chaste reader every reason to feel heart-warmed. This is part of Sterne's genius, to write simultaneously a song of innocence and experience.

Finally, on the matter of small details to be explained, there is something awkward about the "broken and irregular steps" taken by Tristram as he walks softly to his chaise.[37] Purton's conjecture that Tristram carries Maria with him is problematic for logistical reasons, I think, but she is certainly on the right track.[38] In short, there was no time for Tristram and Maria to take a leisurely ride back into town, to the comfort and conviviality of the literal Inn. The need was too great, and Tristram's enthusiasm, too immediate. William Hogarth's portraits of *Before* and *After* provide the conceptual setting.[39] If the "inn" in question is a bawdy double entendre, then Tristram's steps are probably broken and irregular because of a particular discomfort that persists as he hurriedly buttons his pants and retreats from the scene, once the conversation ends and Maria again plays vespers. On more than a related note, female prostitutes are the most expert witnesses in the world at recognizing the peculiar gaits and postures of men who try to walk under such tumid circumstances, and the men themselves, presumably unaware of the extent to which their deportments have been rendered ridiculous, would nonetheless assuredly describe their steps as "broken and irregular."

All of this is to say that the Maria scene in *Tristram Shandy* is not what it appears to be. Or, at minimum, the scene is not what the *Beauties of Sterne* would have us believe it to be. But neither is a pornographic reading of the Maria episode defensible, despite what may seem to be my effort to the contrary, because the Tamar allusion carries with it a level of intricacy and pathos that simply will not yield to the smut-peddler's single entendres. This last point becomes even clearer in *A Sentimental Journey*.

The *Journey*'s Maria

In the film *American Beauty*, Lester Burnham develops an infatuation with his teenage daughter's best friend, Angela.[40] Suffering a midlife crisis, languishing in a bad marriage, Lester daydreams about the romances he might have with the beautiful young woman, only to find himself—near the end of the story—alone with Angela. She happens to be both naked and agreeable. But in a moment of seemingly untimely reflection, Lester rediscovers the idea of fatherhood and so sees in Angela his own daughter, which prompts him to cover her with a blanket and whisper, "Everything's okay." Do we trust Yorick to behave similarly in this type of circumstance? Or, more to the point, does he behave similarly, for this is precisely the kind of situation in which he finds himself with Maria?

Two years have passed, Yorick notes, since Tristram saw her, and in that interval Maria "stray'd as far as Rome, and walk'd round St. Peter's once,—and return'd back," in what is best described as a not-so-sentimental journey.[41] She "travell'd over all Lombardy, without money,—and through the flinty roads of Savoy without shoes:—how she had borne it, and how she had got supported, she could not tell," or—more to the point—would not tell.[42] Here, Sterne invites the logical reader to envision Maria's wanderings, but he provides none of the necessary logistics by which such a journey might occur, requiring us to fill in the missing parts of the incomplete syllogism. Are we to believe, for example, that Maria benefited only from the kindness of strangers, with never a *quid pro quo* attached? Is this how she made the tour, a Good Samaritan around every corner, on every backroad, in every tavern, down every alleyway? If we surmise as much, then we risk putting ourselves in the awkward position of Doctor Pangloss, the self-proclaimed optimist in Voltaire's *Candide* (1759). Maybe in the best of all possible worlds Maria would have blithely wandered only into happy scenarios populated by kind people with pure motives, but "affliction had touched her looks with something that was scarce earthly," Yorick notices, and so we are inclined to infer otherwise.[43] Not that we need to infer the worst. There is no reason to caste too dark of a shadow upon her journey, or pilgrimage, or erotic-romp-prodigal-daughter-morality-tale whatchamacallit. Maria goes by her own volition and returns not that much worse for wear, it seems, though Sterne certainly inscribes in her a palpable melancholy consistent with those who have been disappointed in love. Disappointed more than once, no doubt. But underneath the disillusionment, we also discover in Maria a kind of doggedness that counterbalances her frailty. After all, she survives the journey; or, better still, she transforms the harrowing experience into a flirtatious pretext from which she whispers into Yorick's ear a particularly memorable proverb: "*God tempers the wind*, said Maria, *to the shorn lamb*," to which Yorick ejaculates, "Shorn indeed!"[44]

One part prayer of thanksgiving, one part indecent proposal, Maria's cryptic proverb proves especially useful for our aims, because it cleverly reawakens the Judah-and-Tamar allusion. In the most literal sense, the proverb reminds us of sheep and shears, which Judah thought about as he traveled to Tinmath. That is, he went to shear sheep. En route, of course, he happened upon a conveniently located prostitute and—like Lord Henry Wotton—rationalized that "the only way to get rid of temptation is to yield to it."[45] All of this, I think, is contained in Maria's proverb, along with a second and much bawdier meaning that also reinforces the Judah-and-Tamar motif. Speaking factually, speaking literally, but in a different sense of the literal, Maria has been shorn, or shaved, as was the common practice among the period's female prostitutes, not only for aesthetic and marketing reasons, but also for a decidedly practical reason, that is, to reduce the likelihood of pubic lice. That the merkin industry flourished in eighteenth-century France is a collateral fact worth mentioning, but there is no need further to digress. Maria, through her half-pious, half-erotic proverb, simultaneously talks to Yorick about God and sex. And once we apprehend the bawdy sense, we immediately see that Maria seduces Yorick, or at least attempts to seduce him. In this way, their interaction bears a family resemblance to that scene in W. H. Auden's "Atlantis" where a stripper gently whispers into the young adept's ear, "This is Atlantis, dearie."[46] Maria says much the same thing to Yorick, only with more pathos and a different plan of attack, given that Yorick is anything but a young adept. On the contrary, he is a weathered participant in this type of discourse, but even he seems surprised by Maria's direct approach. And slightly conflicted, or certainly thrilled. Or maybe both.

Yorick's response—"Shorn indeed! and to the quick" is—in the pious sense—a pious response, but in the not-so-pious sense betrays his immediate arousal, recalling that similar moment when Tristram "sprung" out of his chaise to help poor Maria.[47] Additionally, "to the quick" echoes Adriana's notable speech about adultery in *The Comedy of Errors*, when she mistakes for her husband his identical twin, Antipholus: "How dearly would it touch thee to the quick, / Shouldst thou but hear I were licentious / And that this body, consecrate to thee, / By ruffian lust should be contaminate."[48] Sterne's use of Shakespeare is important because it highlights Yorick's moment of conscience. By the *Journey*'s dream logic, Yorick hears Adriana's condemnation of infidelity and, by the principle of substitution, Eliza's condemnation as well. Eliza, to whom Yorick has promised his devotion and for whom Maria is only a temporary substitute. In Adriana's case, the appearance of infidelity is simply that, an appearance, a comic misunderstanding, but the same cannot be said of Yorick's behavior. Rather, the best that can be said is that he thinks of Eliza while having sex with Maria, which is not exactly a triumph of morality. The excuse, "I was thinking of you the entire time," seldom convinces the aggrieved, and yet Yorick attempts to mitigate his conscience by this comedy of metonyms wherein Maria stands in for his actual beloved, who was there in concept, if not in flesh. Such is the reasoning of the semi-regretful adulterer, Yorick included, and Sterne. Indeed, beneath the logic by which Yorick substitutes Maria for Eliza there functions a deeper psychology of prostitution, where we discover Sterne substituting lovers for his wife, Elizabeth. In the biographical sense of the passage, if such a reading is desirable, we might hear in Adriana's "to the quick" a remote echo of Elizabeth's disappointment with Laurence. And if we know Adriana's speech well enough, which I suspect Sterne did, then we may remember that after the talk of licentiousness comes terms like "adulterate blot," "stain'd skin," and "contagion."[49] These are not quite as troubling as Lady Macbeth's "out, damn'd spot," but nor are they the types of things that husbands hope to hear from their wives.[50]

After Yorick and Maria have their moment together, erotic sheep shearing proverb included, Yorick devotes the rest of the scene to another kind of rationalization. He explains to Maria (and to himself) why they cannot go to his cottage, and in these explanations the Judah-and-Tamar allusion once again figures prominently. If they were in England, Yorick initially declares, then he would certainly take Maria to his cottage, feed her, and look after her, in all of her "weaknesses and wanderings."[51] But they are not in England, obviously, never mind the fact that he already promised the cottage to Eliza. This first excuse is flimsy, except on the point that Maria wanders, which is true and also Yorick's way of saying that she cannot be trusted, as if he has room to complain. Nonetheless, Yorick prepares to say goodbye; he lays the initial groundwork for a departure, and once their business is finished, he delivers a second and more viable excuse for why they cannot go to his cottage:

> So much was there about her of all that the heart wishes, or the eyes look for in a woman, that could the traces be ever worn out of her brain, and those of Eliza out of mine, she should *not only eat of my bread and drink of my own cup*, but Maria should lie in my bosom, and be unto me as a daughter.[52]

At this point, the attentive reader should detect in Yorick's subjunctive-mood machinations a logic of the sort that arrives after the fact but before the final settlement of a sexual liaison. And we are woefully mistaken, too, if we think that Maria wants to go with him to his cottage, or to any cottage, for that matter. Rather, she waits patiently for Yorick to wax grandiloquent, and then she happily accompanies him to town on the very clear promise that he will not, under any circumstance, take her anywhere. The attentive reader should also detect in Yorick's cottage-and-daughter talk a dissonant note; at best, Yorick says a strange thing, and—at worst—something glaringly inappropriate, given that he admits a sexual attraction to Maria in the very same sentence. McGlynn, for example, describes the daughter reference as a "statement that *The New Yorker* would likely categorize in its Uh Huh Department," which sounds about right.[53] But the reason why it is right proves more difficult to explain, largely because Sterne cleverly hides the bawdry behind a tender Bible verse, 2 Samuel 12:3, thus allowing the innocent reader to discover no bawdry at all.

Does Yorick—without irony, without innuendo—allude to 2 Samuel 12:3 in order to declare his fatherly intensions toward Maria? In the verse, the prophet Nathan tells King David a parable about a poor man who "had nothing except one little ewe lamb he had bought. He raised it, and it grew up with him and his children. It shared his food, drank from his cup and even slept in his arms. It was like a daughter to him."[54] Importantly, Nathan makes no mention of the poor man's wife, probably indicating that she had died. The ewe, therefore, functions as a substitutionary companion, not in the carnal sense, but rather in the emotional sense; that is, the man in Nathan's parable transfers his affections onto the lamb, in what might be described as the antithesis of scapegoating.[55] Similarly, Yorick wants us to believe that he would transfer the same type of fatherly affection onto Maria, the ewe lamb in this metaphor, if they were in England, of course, and if she could forget the other lovers to whom she is devoted, and, finally, if he could forget Eliza. This hypothetical series of events seems improbable, but even if possible, we still confront the problem of Yorick's sexual attraction to Maria. To believe that he could repress such an attraction so that she could be his "daughter" strains credulity. Put differently, Yorick's effort to connect his cottage-and-daughter talk to 2 Samuel 12:3 is a ruse. He has another biblical daughter in mind.

Is it Ruth? We might be tempted quite naturally to conclude that Ruth is the real subject of Yorick's "daughter" talk, if for no other reason than the style in which Sterne casts *A Sentimental Journey*. He regularly imitates the book of Ruth, as Vicesimus Knox—one of Sterne's early critics—rightly noticed:

> It is easy to see that the writer of so many tender and simple passages had imitated the delightful book of Ruth. With what pleasure did a man of his feeling read, "Entreat me not to leave thee, or to return from following after thee; for whither thou goest, I will go; and where thou lodgest, I will lodge; thy people shall be my people, and thy God my God; where thou diest will I die, and there will I be buried." Sterne stole the very spirit of this passage, and indeed all of the fine strokes of tenderness, and many a one there is, in a book which is often laid aside by polite scholars as absurd and obsolete.[56]

This is the same Vicesimus Knox, incidentally, who described Sterne as "the grand promoter of adultery, and every species of illicit commerce," adding that Sterne's "wit" was "of the lowest kind," his character, "greatly reprehensible," and his *A Sentimental Journey*, "pernicious."[57] He also blamed Sterne for England's rising divorce rate, but on the question of the *Journey*'s stylistic influence, Knox was absolutely right. And in defense of other attempts to connect Maria to Ruth, we might once again remember that Boaz called Ruth his "daughter" before he called her his "wife." The May-to-December aspect of the Ruth–Boaz romance reminds us of Maria as well, but if Maria really were to be understood as a Ruth figure, and Yorick, Boaz, then he would have taken her to the cottage and promptly married her. This does not happen. Ergo, we find ourselves in a different storyline, one that nonetheless involves a biblical daughter touched by tragedy, marked by promiscuity, connected to the book of Ruth, but not Ruth, childless, and in the company of an older man who struggles with sexual propriety. This is Tamar. Other biblical women also inform Maria's aura, undoubtedly, as is the nature of Sterne's richly layered writing, and they, too, should be mentioned: the Samaritan woman at the well in John 4, to whom Christ says, "Thou hast had five husbands"; the Shunamitte woman from 2 Kings 4, childless until blessed by the prophet Elisha; the woman crying in the wilderness in 2 Esdras 10, to whom Yorick alludes earlier in the *Journey*; Gomer from Hosea 1–3, the wandering prostitute; Mary Magdalen, the reformed prostitute.[58] And there are influences beyond the Bible as well: Albrecht Dürer's *Melancholia*, who sits "with her elbow in her lap, and her head leaning on one side within her hand"; Shakespeare's Ophelia, who has olive leaves "twisted a little fantastically" in her hair; Virgil's Dido, who loved boldly.[59] But behind all of these iconic characters sits Tamar, majestic, alone on the side of road, pretending to be a prostitute and awaiting her destiny: Tamar, Rahab, Ruth, Bathsheba, who is rightly called Uriah's wife, and Saint Mary the Virgin.[60]

If Maria functions as a Tamar figure, then we might reasonably wonder—perhaps as an afterthought—where Onan appears in the *Journey*, besides in the form of those inquisitive readers who accompany Yorick on his travels. Indeed, Onan might be omnipresent as a background character, but Sterne recalls him most interestingly in two ways. First are the various motions and commotions throughout the *Journey*, some more obviously colored by a masturbatory innuendo than others, from the galloping chaise ride outside of Nampont to the "undescribable emotions" felt by Yorick as he contemplates Maria, which recall the "multiple emotions" felt by Parson Tickletext as he contemplates the eroticism of Richardson's *Pamela*.[61] Second, more specifically, is the Maria scene's invocation, where "Nature pours her abundance into every one's lap," while Yorick observes a countryside "pregnant with adventure."[62] The proximity of laps, abundant pouring, and talk of pregnancy are enough to warrant a conjecture about *coitus interruptus*. The same might be said of Tristram's nearly identical description in volume 7, where "nature pours out all her abundance, &c.," emphasis on the ambiguity of "&c.," which Yorick then replaces with "lap."[63] Tristram, like Yorick, celebrates a fertile landscape, but the specter of infertility also lingers in the scene, either in the form of masturbation or interrupted sex, both of which prefigure Maria—a young woman with several sexual experiences but no children. Another and related reason why Maria remains childless might be discovered in the *Tristram* scene where she "put[s] the pipe to her mouth" and plays vespers. Attentive readers presumably remember it, just as we remember the queen of Navarre's very sudden "Ave Maria" in the middle of her meditation on "whiskers."[64] In brief, and perhaps to state the obvious, we need not doubt that Sterne makes room in his satires for both Onan and religious habits.

As for Judah archetypes beyond Yorick, the German in Nampont comes readily to mind. Before Maria, Yorick and La Fleur encounter a German who laments his dead ass, but underneath that grief is a more substantial one. He lost two of his three sons to small-pox, at which point he made a not-so-rash vow to God: he would go on a pilgrimage to St. James in Spain, if his third son were to be spared. The boy lived, and so we encounter the German on his way back home, when his ass finally broke down and died, causing him to experience—perhaps for the first time—feelings of the profoundest sorrow: he mourns not only his donkey but also his two sons. Of the German's wife we know nothing, it should be added, except that she is absent, which in this case probably suggests her death and so further punctuates the German's role as a Judah archetype. As such, he foreshadows the Maria scene, specifically on the matter of emotional transference. Just as the German projects his affection onto his donkey, so too Maria projects her affection onto Sylvio.[65] Both take comfort in substitutions for the beloved, a trope in which Yorick also participates, once we see Madame de L***, the *fille de chambre*, the *grisette*, Maria, etcetera, as temporary substitutions for Eliza. We might say the same of Sterne, too, whose extramarital affairs operate as the autobiographical backdrop against which Yorick's substitutionary romances unfold. That the German is also willing to substitute a woman for his absent beloved is not an unreasonable inference on our part, given the *Journey*'s tenor, and once we make such a guess, a very interesting question arises: Did the German version of Judah travel through Moulins? Because Nampont is on the northern-most pilgrimage route, his return trip would not have brought him there, but he may have taken the well-worn southern route on his way to St. James, through Moulins, especially if the climate required it. In other words, we might rationally speculate that the German met Maria, allowing them both to engage in projection, transference, and substitution, or—more concisely phrased—prostitution. And because travelers on pilgrimages have a moral duty to travel light, with only the bare essentials in tow, the German may not have had a proper payment in hand, and so he would have left behind some sort of collateral. A pearl earring, for example, or possibly a handkerchief.

Conclusion

Sex is one of the most beautiful, natural, and wholesome things that money can buy. Such is the sentiment in the Maria episodes, which are best read as gentle satires. The main target: respectable middle-aged men who—for convoluted reasons—find themselves with young prostitutes. And if this target sounds familiar to Sterne, it should. In a self-deprecating way, he uses the Maria scenes to analyze his own stories of temptation, which begin with thoughts of benevolence, chivalry, and other high-minded ideals, all of which fly out the window as soon as the Marias of the world talk about their shorn lambs. Of course, this is not to conflate Tristram and Yorick with Sterne. Rather, these characters function as Sterne's thinly disguised half-alter-egos, examples of older men who prove to be more easily seducible than they might have imagined themselves to be. At least Odysseus had the foresight to tie himself to the mast of his ship, ensuring that he would not succumb to the sirens' song. Tristram and Yorick take no such measures, and nor does Sterne, it seems, which speaks to the moral crux of the Maria episodes: conscience is a fickle thing. It goes on sabbatical; it goes on hiatus, often at those times when it is needed most. "We trust that we have a good conscience," Paul writes in Hebrews and Sterne repeats in his sermon on the topic, but that trust is woefully misplaced at times, as the Maria scenes expertly illustrate.[66] We fool ourselves more readily than we think.

What, then, of Tamar's role in Sterne's tragi-comical Maria episodes? For our purposes, the Tamar allusion helpfully confirms an experienced reading. That is, it confirms prostitution and so also participates in Sterne's critique of conscience as a reliable guide. This is to assume that Tristram and Yorick only half-intended to have sex with Maria, but those half-intensions persisted until they were the only intensions that remained, at which point Tristram and Yorick got what they bargained for. The same might be said of Judah, who did not plan to have sex with a prostitute, but when presented with a real opportunity, when the hypothetical became not only conceivable but also convenient, he quickly abandoned his scruples. Such is the human condition. And we might add to this a second failure on Judah's part: he could not see his own daughter-in-law in the young prostitute's posture. Or, put differently, he failed to empathize and so did not ask those fatherly questions that generate compassion. What were her circumstances? Who missed her, and whom did she miss? Who scanned the horizon for any indication of her return?[67] Such inquiries are seldom made in the middle of illicit commerce, and we know why: nothing ruins pornography like real sentiment. There is never a right time or proper measure by which to discover the dreams and disappointments of prostitutes, and worse still are the family backstories: parents in denial who believe their daughters to have found work in the city as seamstresses, which is Hogarth's vision in *A Harlot's Progress*; or broken-hearted mothers and fathers who imagine worst-case scenarios and wait restlessly for unwanted news.[68] This is Sterne's vision in the second Maria episode, where any indecent desire for a Fanny Hill-style adventure quickly gives way to the humanizing force of Sterne's literary genius.[69] And yet for all of the genuine sentiment that Yorick feels toward Maria and her parents, and for all of the discernment we expect from a priest who sees "*Religion* mixing in the dance," the illicit commerce nonetheless proceeds.[70] Original sin, a clever theologian once quipped, is the only provable part of Christian doctrine.

Finally, and in defense of my critics, perhaps I have simply read too much into the Maria scenes, or at least I am vulnerable to that charge. Maybe I look like Benedick toward the end of *Much Ado about Nothing*: "There's a double meaning in that," he says, as he grasps at straws, trying to discern a secret message in Beatrice's curt dinner invitation, which is not even her invitation exactly, but rather her uncle's as delivered through her: "Against my will I am sent to bid you come in to dinner."[71] We laugh, of course, as we see Benedick search for the double entendre, and the scene is funny precisely because he does not find it. But as it happens, and to our deeper amusement still, there is—in fact—a double meaning buried in Beatrice's reluctant dinner invitation and couched more broadly in Shakespeare's joke about a man who fails to find a double meaning. "He hath an excellent stomach," Beatrice declares of Benedick early in the play, when she hears of his shooting exploits and, by implication, his sexual exploits.[72] This piques her curiosity, though she dare not say so directly, and so she notes instead his excellent stomach, or sexual appetite, depending, which puts us on the path of food-and-sex metaphors, of which her reluctant-but-not-so-reluctant dinner invitation is one. When in the presence of Shakespeare, we are better served to err on the side of too much meaning, not too little. And while there is certainly a danger of reading too much into Sterne, the greater danger—I think—is the same as it is with Shakespeare, and this is to find too little. Sometimes a cigar is just a cigar, and sometimes a goat is just a goat. Maybe Maria's goat is of that kind, and Yorick, a benevolent priest, Tristram, a concerned traveler, even a Good Samaritan, and Maria, an innocent victim of circumstance. We can leave it there. Sentimental stories for sentimental readers. Balm in Gilead. But behind the veil of these innocent readings lurks a more sordid affair, I believe, where compromised people behave very imperfectly in order—somehow—to cope with loss. Whether or not Sterne provides the best answer for those who find themselves in the company of prostitutes is a separate question, and one I certainly do not aim to answer here. What I do know is that Sterne is utterly believable. Indeed, his self-critical satires remind me of something C.S. Lewis once said: "Ever since I served as an infantryman in the First World War, I have had a great dislike of people who, themselves in ease and safety, issue exhortations to men in the front line. As a result I have a reluctance to say much about temptations to which I myself am not exposed."[73] These are wise words, and Sterne—I think—demonstrates the same wisdom. I will listen to his exhortations.

5

Otherworldly Yorick

Parson Yorick dies in 1748, by the Shandean timeline, and "lies buried in a corner of his church-yard."[1] On that same timeline, "Yorick" suddenly reappears in 1763, as if conjured by a sorcerer. And so begins his sentimental journey, brimming with redemptive double entendres and biblical truths of the sort that grave priests do not know. By any normal standard, we confront a blatant chronological incongruity, a Yorick-died-and-therefore-how-can-he-go-to-France problem. But even the earliest critics took the problem in stride. They perceived in the *Journey*'s Yorick not a resurrected corpse but rather a reimagined persona, a new literary vehicle through whom Sterne expounded timely philosophical arguments. That is, *Tristram*'s Yorick and the *Journey*'s Yorick were to be seen as different characters, even though they looked alike and had, it seemed, the same knowledge of the Shandyverse. Nevertheless, two Yoricks are better than one, especially if one dies in 1748.

Such was the first effort to reconcile the old with the new Yorick, and the only effort, truly, insofar as the modern critics inherit this two-Yoricks solution and perpetuate it, as in Elizabeth Kraft's lucid explanation:

> Readers would have realized [that] the Yorick who narrates *A Sentimental Journey* was a flexible mask in Sterne's hands, rather than a consistent character, and while associations with a certain kind of personality—spontaneous, impulsive, sympathetic, and impatience with self-justification—would have certainly informed the first reading of *A Sentimental Journey*, no identification with the biographical details of Yorick's life as readers knew it from Sterne's earlier work would have been expected.[2]

Others agree, from Arthur Cash and Melvyn New to Thomas Keymer, for example, who speaks of Yorick's "personae," or Tim Parnell, who describes the *Journey*'s Yorick as another of Sterne's "playfully donned social masks."[3] And if not two Yoricks, then more. John Stedmond counts as a third version the *Journal*'s Yorick, while Elizabeth Goodhue declares more recently that "no two of the rhetorical Yoricks are identical," though exactly how many she tallies we are not certain.[4] Maybe four: *Tristram*'s, the *Sermons*', the *Journey*'s, and the *Journal*'s. Or five, if we add Sterne, who occasionally referred to himself as Yorick at dinner parties, but Sterne lived in our world and should therefore be treated differently, I think, not as a literary character but rather as an author who sporadically played a literary character. And as far as the *Sermons*' and the *Journal*'s Yoricks are concerned, we are best served to treat them as extensions of their respective Yoricks from *Tristram* and the *Journey*, as Sterne does, bringing us back to the original problem of two distinct Yoricks. Regardless of how one counts Yoricks, however, this much should be abundantly clear: a strong consensus supports the idea that more than one Yorick exists in the Shandyverse. Indeed, so strong is the consensus that it functions as a presupposition, which is to say that a unified Yorick theory seems out of the question.

And, certainly, the parson's death makes awkward any effort to argue that the *Journey*'s Yorick is *Tristram*'s Yorick, which is my conjectural claim, with the caveat that the other Yoricks are one and the same, too. In other words, there is only one Yorick in Sterne's literary cosmos, the priest we first meet in *Tristram Shandy*, discover further through *The Sermons*, and then—to our genuine surprise—encounter again as the *Journey*'s amiable narrator. And if the *Bramine's Journal* is to be taken as proper literature, we find the same Yorick there, also. But such a unified character proves difficult to imagine, unless he staged his own death, a scenario for which I have found no evidence. In fact, the opposite is the case; we have every reason to believe that Yorick died. If he is to be the same character throughout, we must therefore pursue a different line of enquiry, and what I have in mind, in particular, requires a temporary suspension of disbelief: namely, perhaps the *Journey*'s Yorick is a ghost. A fleshy ghost, to be sure, which has ample precedence in the period's ghost literature, but a ghost nonetheless. Sterne provides intriguing evidence to this end, in the works themselves and in the letters. Moreover, the Yorick-as-ghost thesis perfectly complements the *Journey*'s philosophical project, which is to repudiate Baron d'Holbach and his salon of atheists, all of whom described humans as complex machines.[5] Yorick's ghost suggests otherwise, adamantly, and thus stands as a testament to Sterne's supernaturalism, much like the king's ghost in *Hamlet* testifies to Shakespeare's supernaturalism, similarly confirming a world beyond death, however ambiguous it might be. Finally, perhaps most importantly from the standpoint of narrative structure, the Yorick-as-ghost thesis solves one of the deepest Shandean riddles, that of the timeline, which Sterne impeccably preserves in the *Journey*, with the dramatic exception of Yorick. Maria is slightly older, Tristram as well, and we find ourselves nostalgically remembering the old times, made all the more poignant by Uncle Toby's unexpected death.[6] Everything proceeds cogently except for the presence of Yorick, who remains decidedly out of synchronicity insofar as he should be dead. In comes the ghost, at which point the problem of discontinuity vanishes entirely. We discover instead that Yorick is not gone but only transformed, or, more precisely, undergoing transformation. Eastern Orthodox priests talk about "the final theosis," that journey of purification through the twilight kingdom between death and Heaven, which is not exactly Purgatory, nor is it Abraham's Bosom, though it contains elements of both, and an element, too, of the Greek and Roman underworlds, where Aeneas meets Dido and weeps. The Yorick we encounter in the *Journey* partly travels in this otherworldly realm, and partly carries it with him, giving the narrative a dream-like atmosphere, akin to the quality we discover in David Lynch's *Mulholland Drive*, for instance, or René Magritte's *A Modern Venus*. All of this is to say that the Yorick-as-ghost thesis holds much explanatory power. It opens a portal to the *Journey*'s fantastic dimensions, and, for adventuresome travelers, promises a new route through Sterne's sentimental masterpiece.

Some Evidence

Sterne will not admit that the *Journey*'s Yorick is a ghost. No manicules point to confessions, but we do find evidence. Early in *Tristram Shandy*, "Yorick's ghost" haunts his own gravesite, lingering, watching passersby rehearse—"in plaintive tones"—that monumental inscription carved into the marble: "A las poor YORICK."[7] In volume 2, the ghost reappears, or at least the idea of it. After recounting Yorick's tragic death and unjust reputation, Tristram delivers to the world the sermon on conscience, in an effort (he assures us) to "give rest to Yorick's ghost," who "the country-people" and "some others" believe "still walks."[8] Taken together, these references posit a ghostly Yorick beyond the realm of mere metaphor, that is, beyond the purely figurative. Not that the figurative is wrong. Sterne writes on many levels, and Yorick haunts *Tristram* in the figurative sense as well, evoking progressively intense feelings of nostalgia as we get to know him better through Tristram's retrospective narrative. And the better we know him, the more intimately we suffer his loss. But a literal ghost also persists, if Tristram is to be believed, and if not Tristram, then the country people and some others. How to interpret the ghost is a separate matter, of course, but to treat him only as a figment of the imagination seems overly simplistic, not to mention unkind.

Are we therefore to read *Tristram Shandy* as a ghost story? I would not go that far, but if the ghost in question were to tell a sentimental tale of his own, then what would that be called, if not a sentimental ghost story?

Yorick's ghost also haunts the *Bramine's Journal*, Sterne's difficult-to-categorize literary experiment. Straightforwardly, it is a series of maudlin letters by which the dying Sterne romances Eliza Draper, a married woman with whom he had an emotional affair, at minimum.[9] But not so straightforwardly, the *Journal* functions as a creative notebook wherein Sterne—through Yorick—roughly drafts some of the *Journey*'s deepest dream logic, and this is where the ghost comes into play. Among the set pieces and habnabbery, Sterne invents a ghost dimension, a shadowland between worlds with "secret walkways, encircled by a myrtle grove."[10] Here, the ghostly priest stirs. Indeed, the *Journal*'s Yorick refers to himself as an ethereal "Spirit."[11] He has a "gawsy constitution," and at a key moment, perhaps the crescendo, he plays the role of Hamlet's ghostly father, imploring Eliza not to forget him:

> 29th and 30th confined to my bed—so emaciated, and unlike what I was, I could scarse be angry with thee Eliza, if thou Could not remember me, did heaven send me across thy way—Alas! Poor Yorick!—"*remember thee! Pale Ghost—remember thee—while Memory holds a seat in this distracted World—Remember thee,*"— Yes, from the table of her Memory, shall just Eliza wipe away all trivial men—& leave a throne for Yorick—adieu dear constant Girl—adieu—adieu.—& Remember my Truth and eternal fidelity Remember how I Love—remember What I suffer.—Thou art mine Eliza by Purchace—had I not earned thee with a better price.[12]

Sterne's bad health looms in the background of the scene, obviously, while in the foreground Yorick, dressed in the ectoplasmic garb of the king's ghost, declares his love for Eliza. She very temporarily plays Hamlet, in this play within a play, but the *Hamlet* allusion quickly collapses, and this for good reason. If *Hamlet*'s structure were to be carried forward in the *Journal*, beyond the simple entreaty to remember, then the relationship between Yorick and Eliza would remind us not of the king's ghost and Hamlet but rather of Claudius and Gertrude, early on. A clandestine love affair, an inconvenient husband, etcetera. And while Yorick seems an unlikely candidate for a murder plot, he nonetheless daydreams of a widowed Eliza, and reminds her as well of his imaginative pilgrimages to her temple, as he lies restless in bed, unable to sleep, reminiscent of Trim and the Beguine nurse, for example, or perhaps those nuns who toss and turn all night while thinking of Hafen Slawkenbergius's nose, and then get up in the morning "like so many ghosts."[13] In other words, Sterne decides not to carry the *Hamlet* subtext too far in the *Journal* because Shakespeare's plot does not lend itself easily to lovesick sentimentalism. At the same time, he carries the *Hamlet* allusion far enough to remind us of Yorick's ghostliness and, too, to clarify that we find ourselves in an otherworldly atmosphere, séance-like, theosophical.[14] Nor should the cleverness of the scene as it relates to Sterne's authorship go unnoticed, because Sterne's ghost likewise haunts the page: Yorick the ghost plays a ghost, and the author's spirit hovers behind him, prompting us to remember that the dead continue to speak their truths through books, and continue to speak their confessions through books as well, as the case might be.

Exactly what the remainder of this passage means is more difficult to say. The thou-art-mine expostulation most likely recalls Ruth 4:10, where Boaz purchases some land and Ruth, the Moabite. She gives birth to Obed, who leads to David and, farther down the genealogy, Jesus of Nazareth. But the expostulation may just as easily recall the thou-art-mine refrains from Exodus 2 and Isaiah 43. Here, God declares eternal fidelity to Israel, foreshadowing Revelation 21—the wedding at the end of time. In either case, or both cases, Yorick speaks prophetically. He moves from *Hamlet*'s ghostly style to a biblical–anagogical register, elevating Eliza in the process to the status of an icon. She becomes a repository for Yorick's hopes and desires, and he, an acolyte projecting himself through the astral plane and into Eliza's dream consciousness. Of course, all of this happens in glimpses and partial visions; Yorick shores these fragments against his ruin.

Nothing in the *Journal* is full-fledged, nor will the half-melancholy *Hamlet*-to-Ruth scenario confirm Yorick's standing as a ghost, but it does create an otherworldly aura, convincingly so, which I take as circumstantial evidence. In other words, the *Journal* is precisely the sort of place that we would expect to find a ghost, however unlikely such ghost encounters happen to be.

The Letters also contain intriguing ghost references, one of which—in particular—stands out. Sterne writes to his banker friend Robert Foley in 1764, about the same time he was finishing volumes 7 and 8 of *Tristram Shandy*, and within the letter he imagines himself to be a fleshy ghost:

> When you have got to your fireside, and into your arm-chair (and by the by, have another to spare for a friend), and are so much a sovereign as to sit in your furr'd cap (if you like it, tho' I should not, for a man's ideas are at least the cleaner for being dress'd decently), why then it will be a miracle if I do not glide in like a ghost upon you—and in a very unghost-like fashion help you off with a bottle of your best wine.[15]

The passage might just as easily have appeared in *Tristram*, given the attention to clothing and composition, the "furr'd cap" bawdry, and the overall playfulness. In fact, if Sterne were to become a ghost, we would imagine nothing less from him than a puckish, wine-drinking spirit like this one. And if wine, then why not romance? That is, Sterne's lively ghost rejects the grave tenets of ghostliness, and when we take some poetic license and envision the fleshy ghost in other circumstances, we begin to appreciate the philosophical force behind Sterne's quip. It is, I think, another statement against Gnosticism, the supposedly dignified dream of pure spirituality, which promises a future unencumbered by the material pleasures of chocolate, laughter, and sex. An idea anathema to Christian metaphysics. Such are the "Platonics" against whom Swift rails in *The Mechanical Operation of the Spirit* (1704), those philosophers whose heads float in the clouds but whose bodies betray another set of motives entirely.[16] "The root is in the earth," Swift's manic narrator notices, in a double entendre that echoes Christ's parable of the sower, only with a libidinous twist, and Sterne's gliding ghost essentially reminds us of the same.[17] The body is part of the equation, in this life and the next. Paradise brings with it a profound physicality, by the doctrines of traditional Christianity, and this includes the idea of a glorified new body capable of pleasures that would make even the most ambitious of earthy hedonists blush. A torrent of voluptuousness, to borrow C.S. Lewis's phrase.[18] Of course, Sterne's fleshy ghost has not yet arrived at such a torrent; he is too busy pilfering wine and working out his own salvation, but as an emblem of hope in a future to come, Sterne's buoyant specter strikes much closer to the mark than those lethargic characters who sit on clouds and play harps for all eternity. Some Heaven, that. A *New Yorker* cartoon displays exactly such a scene, where one character looks at another with an expression on his face of numb insensibility. The caption: "I always figured Hell would be less ironic."[19] More to the point at hand, the fleshy-ghost quip gives us a peek into the imaginative process by which Sterne developed a full-fledged ghostly Yorick for the *Journey*. It is to be seen as an early experiment, I believe, and a successful one, insofar as Sterne rightly envisions a ghost who behaves in a decidedly "unghost-like fashion."

Soon after Sterne began to compose the fleshy-ghost letter to Foley, he fell ill. We know this because of a follow-up remark in the letter's conclusion, dated ten days later, January 15. Here, Sterne alludes to his earlier "liberty" with ghosts, but—in Shandean fashion—he also interrupts himself with a satirical digression:

> It does not happen every day that a letter begun in the most perfect health should be concluded in the greatest weakness—I wish the vulgar high and low do not say it was a judgement upon me for taking all this liberty with *ghosts*—Be it as it may—I took a ride

when the first part of this was wrote toward Perenas—and returned home in a shivering fit, though I ought to have been in a fever, for I had tired my beast; and he was as unmovable as Don Quixote's wooden horse, and my arm was half dislocated in whipping him— This quoth I is inhuman—No, says a peasant on foot behind me, I'll drive him home—so he laid on his posterior, but twas needless— as his face was turned toward Montpellier he began to trot.—But to return, this fever has confined me ten days in my bed—I have suffered in this scuffle with death terribly—but unless the spirit of prophecy deceive me—I shall not die but live.[20]

The Cervantes allusion will remind attentive readers of Margarita and the abbess of Andoüillets, those nuns (and lovers) who resort to profane language in order to move stubborn mules up a hill, but Sterne's primary aim in the letter lies elsewhere.[21] Specifically, he conveys his bad health, all the while demonstrating enough health to be witty, which he and Foley find reassuring, presumably: unless deceived by the "spirit of prophecy," he "shall not die." Apparently, however, "the vulgar high and low" think otherwise, or at least they imagine Sterne to have put himself at risk by taking liberty with ghosts. How should we interpret such a diagnosis? And, perhaps just as pressingly, does Sterne believe it? The vulgar-high-and-low comment carries a dismissive-enough tone to cause skepticism, if this is Sterne's point, but the remark is not entirely dismissive, which leads to a genuine enquiry about the extent to which writers should make merry with ghosts. In the notes, New and de Voogd propose as much: "It is noteworthy that when Sterne returns to this letter ten days later, he suggests his illness might be retribution for his play with 'ghost,' rather than with 'furr'd cap.'"[22] Their implication is that Sterne worried more about occultism than erotica in terms of heresy, which is wholly true. Still, I doubt that he felt any genuine regret about his fleshy ghost banter, because if he had, then the Cervantes digression would not have come so easily. Rather, what we see in Sterne's comment about the "vulgar high and low" is a writer who considers the proper limits of ghost invocations. He does this, I speculate, because he thinks about how best to conjure up Yorick's ghost for the *Journey*, and, as a conscientious priest, he wanted very much to avoid the role of Endor's witch, or John Dee and Edward Kelly in the graveyard.[23] That is, Sterne did not want an author-as-necromancer metaphor to follow him into the *Journey*, just as Yorick—in the *Journal*—did not want Eliza to see his presence as the work of a "Dreamer of Dreams in the Scriptural Language," a phrase borrowed from Jeremiah 23 and meant to connote the practice of unlawful magic.[24] Ergo, Sterne experiments in the letters and *Journal* with the lawful means by which to deliver a fleshy ghost. At the same time, he formulates a plan to resurrect Yorick and send him on a trip to France, though "resurrect" is not exactly the right word.[25] "Invoke" seems better, or "summons." In either case, that Sterne thinks about fleshy ghosts as he begins in earnest to draft the *Journey* is more than coincidental.

Three years later, in December of 1767, Sterne provides another ghost reference in an uneventful letter to his friends Anne and William James, who expect him for a visit. "Youl see Me enter like a Ghost," he remarks, telling them "beforehand" so that they might not "be frightened."[26] In this case, Sterne nonchalantly uses a ghost metaphor to describe his own failing health. Several kinds of metaphors would have served the purpose, and so the ghost image once more demonstrates a state of mind. Moreover, the casualness of the remark likely confirms that Sterne did not fret over his earlier fleshy-ghost banter. As a general rule, those who fret over such things find different analogies. Instead, he simply carries on with talk of apparitions, unconcerned—it seems—about the possible preternatural consequences.

Finally, we find provocative evidence of Yorick's ghost in the *Journey* itself, though the evidence requires a certain capacity for dream logic, unless we take the narrator at face value to be who he says he is. If so, then the ghost is splendidly obvious. The most striking clue for those who need more convincing, however, appears in the Paris "Fragment." Here, La Fleur finds for Yorick some butter on a currant leaf, and then places both on a piece of "waste paper" that doubles as a plate.[27] After the butter is gone, Yorick reads the waste paper, that is, the literary fragment written "in the old French of Rabelais's time."[28] As we read alongside Yorick, imagining the half-familiar streets and strange passageways, we find ourselves suddenly transported into a prophetic dream, which becomes clear (or as clear as these things can be) upon our unexpected arrival in a bedroom chamber. It is "dismantled of everything but a long military pike,—a breastplate,—a rusty old sword, and bandoleer, hung up, equidistant, in four different places against the wall."[29] And in the bed lies an old man, ready to tell a story. On one level, Sterne obviously pays homage to Rabelais and Cervantes, the second of whom is called to mind through the wall decorations, Don Quixote's tackle and trim. But the scene has a haunting familiarity about it for another reason as well. In another form, in another life, it is Yorick's deathbed scene from *Tristram Shandy*, volume 1. Indeed, we find ourselves in the very same room, only now the room has been transmogrified through the high rhetoric of a dream revelation. In the bed, we discover Yorick, and by reading the Paris "Fragment," Yorick discovers Yorick; he picks up his own skull, figuratively speaking, and ponders mortality. I should add, quickly, that Sterne pays homage as well to Shakespeare in the passage. He very cleverly reconfigures *Hamlet*'s graveyard scene, especially that nostalgic moment when Hamlet holds Yorick's skull and remembers the old days. In an act of satirical genius, Sterne takes this tragic source material and translates it into a bittersweet comedy: after finishing some butter, Yorick surveys the story of his own death, or at least most of it, absent the final page. The "Fragment" ends at precisely that moment when the notary is prepared to record the old man's final adventure. And perhaps it goes without saying, then, that another layer of cleverness also pervades the passage, insofar as it functions as an emblem of the *Journey* itself. Exactly like the Paris "Fragment," the *Journey* ends dramatically and in mid-stride, leaving readers highly amused and certainly disoriented. In other words, the "Fragment" is a play within the play of the *Journey*, a fractured form within a fractured form. And its conclusion, true to form, elicits in Yorick the same response that the *Journey*'s conclusion elicits in us: "Where is the rest of it, La Fleur?"[30]

Sterne imagines a ghostly Yorick, directly in *Tristram Shandy* and the *Journal*, and either indirectly or astoundingly directly in the *Journey*, depending. The remarks in the *Letters*, I think, further reveal a writer who tests the comic import and metaphysical consequences of a fleshy ghost. And behind the literary experiments, of course, we find a satirist who senses his own mortality. Sterne knows that he—soon enough—will be a ghost. That said, I envision objections to the ghost thesis, three of which seem especially pertinent.

Three Objections

First, why would Sterne go through the trouble of inventing a sentimental ghost only to conceal him so deeply under the dark veil of English travel literature? Why hide the ghost? The easy answer is that Sterne simply did not have time to develop more fully the ghost subtext. In the *Journey*'s third volume, for example, he might have planned a scene where Yorick and another ghost mutually frighten each other, or perhaps a scene where Yorick writes a half-completed will and testament to Tristram, only to have the paper fall through a crevice in the floorboards, a mishap as unlikely as Tristram's window circumcision.[31] But even if Sterne had planned to include additional clues in later chapters, they would be just that, strange clues, some hidden in plain sight, and some not. Nothing straightforward would happen, because Sterne happily allows readers to believe otherwise. When critics declared the *Journey* to be his work of redemption, for instance, just as he sardonically suggested it would be, Sterne was pleased to let them believe so, even though the *Journey* abounds with exactly those kinds of double entendres against which the critics so vehemently complained. How any alert reader can find blamelessness in the *Journey*'s grisette-and-gloves scene, for example, is beyond me, and yet Wilbur Cross makes a good point in the opposite direction: "It is all quite innocent provided one takes it so."[32] Sterne, in other words, had no interest in pushing the ghost thesis, but nor do I think he intended to make it entirely subterranean. My hunch is that he aimed at playful ambiguity, akin to Yorick's hope that he would "leave Paris, if it was possible, with all the virtue [he] enter'd it," a cryptogram that satisfies both sentimental and overly inquisitive readers.[33] Similarly, I think it is best to say that a ghost can be seen in the *Journey* if one has eyes to see it; and if one chooses otherwise, then Yorick falls into a different framework, a pilgrim making sentimental progress, as Stout would have it, for example, or Sterne's half-masked persona, or perhaps even Sterne's flirtation with the mechanical philosophy: Yorick's cordiality arrives only after a good dinner; his kindness toward the monk—an attempt to impress a beautiful woman for sexual advantage; his grand declaration that he has a soul, emotive froth brought on by the erotic company of Maria.[34] To be sure, Sterne allows for natural explanations throughout, and yet in the wake of all such explanations, mechanical, religious, psychoanalytic, polemical, biographical, etcetera, a certain unbendable fact continues to haunt the 1763 *Journey*: that is, Yorick died in 1748.

Second, if we are unabashedly to entertain otherworldly explanations, then why privilege the ghost? Why not imagine Yorick to be an incubus, for example, just as Hamlet momentarily imagines the king's ghost to be a "goblin damn'd" disguised as his father?[35] Burton touches upon such creatures in *The Anatomy of Melancholy*, notably, and Sterne would have known about incubi from other sources as well, including much of the period's medical literature on waking dreams and night terrors, not to mention the period's theosophical literature, where dead lovers, or demons cloaked as lovers, find their way back to the living and try to rekindle the flames.[36] If we are to speculate that the *Journey*'s Yorick is preternatural, and if, as some critics have argued, Yorick is far less honorable than he seems, then a darker spirit requires notice. But one discovers in the *Journey* a convincing counterargument to this line of enquiry. That is, an incubus of a sort already makes an appearance, and it is not Yorick. On the contrary, Yorick discerns a demonic presence in his Paris hotel room and finds himself unprepared for its arrival. The scene in question: "The Temptation," where Yorick flirts with a chambermaid whom he had met the previous night and toward whom he had shown nothing but courtesy. On this night, however, he feels something within him "not in strict unison with the lesson of virtue" that he "had given [the chambermaid] the night before," at which point he pretends to search for a card, picks up a pen, sets it back down, feels his hand tremble, and then knows "the devil" is in him.[37] Whatever we may think of demonic entities, we are mistaken to read the devil reference here in merely metaphorical terms, as if to say that Yorick simply describes a state of mind made clear by an antiquated allegory. Rather, Yorick encounters an occult influence and unsuccessfully resists it, I believe, though sentimental readers are certainly welcomed to their view that Yorick conquers his own temptation, however strained such a reading might be.[38] The more likely scenario is that Yorick seduces the maid in the following chapter, "The Conquest," all the while enveloped by a negative spiritual force. Put differently, an incubus informs the *Journey*'s paranormal atmosphere, but the creature is not to be confused with our protagonist.

A third objection: one might wonder why Yorick, if a ghost, feels the need to declare that he has a soul, which happens dramatically in the Maria scene: "I am positive I have a soul; nor can all the books with which materialists have pester'd the world ever convince me to the contrary."[39] At this point, should not Yorick, post-death, simply announce that he is a soul, if he is to say anything about souls? The short answer to this query is probably "yes," though such a phrasing—"I am a soul"—surely invites more problems than it solves. It sounds peculiar, for example, and is somewhat anachronistic to the period's philosophical vocabulary, never mind the risk it poses of luring us into the monism-versus-dualism mire. And if dualism, what kind of dualism, and if not, then whose monism?[40] Inevitably, Leibniz will weigh in with talk of psychophysical parallelism—the theory that mind and body exist in entirely separate spheres and yet are coordinated to be in perfectly harmony with each other, by order of the divine schemata.[41] At which point some might recall the tubster's anti-climax in Swift's *A Tale of a Tub*, the diminuendo wherein he—on the brink of un-riddling the means by which spirit interacts with matter—writes only "*Hic multa ... desiderantur*," here much is wanting.[42] Granted, such speculative discourses can excite the imagination, especially if Walter and Toby are in the room, but, as it stands, we only have Yorick to ponder the mind–body problem, and he lacks the patience required for such casuistic endeavors, not to mention the fact that he has pressing problems of his own, in this case Maria's wiles and the soon-to-be shared hotel room with the lady and her chambermaid. That said, Yorick might certainly describe himself as such, as being a soul (versus having a soul), but cannot we all say the same? The living are fleshy souls as much as the dead, with the caveat that the dead have died and are thus of a different constitution, but fleshy nevertheless, at least by the tenets of Sterne's sensible Christianity.

Perhaps, however, I have sidestepped the deeper query behind the query. Does Yorick know who and where he is? On those questions, we might safely infer that Yorick has not yet found the most precise language by which to describe himself, a fact signaled earlier when he observes the following: "There is not a more perplexing affair in life to me than to set about telling anyone who I am."[43] That is, fleshy ghosts do not necessarily have more insight into selfhood than other types of fleshy spirits. And nor is it correct to assume that Yorick knows exactly where he is, ontologically speaking, except that he finds himself in France and facing obstacles, big and small, coincidences that seem too coincidental to be coincidental, and opportunities for kindness of the sort that give life—and afterlife—meaning. And as for the "materialists" who "pester" Yorick and the world with their talk of the man-machine's dignity, why would they not continue to tempt him?[44] We might remember that Lewis, in *The Great Divorce*, has tub-thumping evangelists with bat-like voices fly up to Heaven and preach to the saved, urging them to throw off the shackles of their oppression.[45] Some literary ghosts in Lewis's allegory also fly from Hell not to Heaven but rather to the Earth's libraries, hoping to discover that their books still prove relevant.[46] Regardless, and in summary to the third objection, the ghost thesis merely dictates that Yorick is a fleshy ghost, not that he fully comprehends the implications of his ghosthood, nor that he realizes—in full—what it means to experience final theosis. All we know for sure is that Yorick knows he has a soul. He will not be persuaded otherwise, and was not persuaded otherwise, in fact, even when the very alluring "Madame de V—" suggested it.[47]

Conclusion

Critics have solved the two-Yoricks problem in a shrewd way, and this is to treat it as no problem at all. More than one Yorick exists, we are told, and that is that. Exactly how many roam the countryside, and to what end, are questions for the psychoanalyst. On the contrary,

I suggest a simple alternative, a unified Yorick theory, which resolves the otherwise insurmountable problem of chronological coherence, and which requires only that we see the *Journey*'s Yorick as a fleshy ghost. Happily, Sterne provides evidence to this end, enough to be persuasive, I think, but not enough to make the ghost so obvious that readers lack a prerogative to believe otherwise, if they so choose. In other words, Dr. Eustace's walking stick has several handles, one of which carries us into the *Journey*'s ghost world.[48] My task, then, has been to demonstrate the cogency of that world, not its preeminence. One need not see the ghost in order to be moved by Sterne's sentiments, for example, nor must we see the ghost in order to appreciate the satire, though the comedy takes on added layers of wit and pleasure if we do. And I find others advantages, too, of detecting the *Journey*'s Yorick as a ghost, upon which—in conclusion—I will expound.

First, the ghost thesis invites us to revisit Sterne's literary influences. The difficult question is what to include as relevant for our purposes. From the Old Testament, Sterne most obviously draws upon the story of Samuel's ghost, who delivers bad news to Saul and also surprises the Witch of Endor.[49] She expected a demon, not a man. From the New Testament, Sterne presumably finds Moses, who appears as something of a ghost alongside Elijah and Christ in Matthew 17, the Transfiguration, though exactly how he got there remains a point of ambiguity.[50] We might also look to the literary séance, if rethinking source material. Lucian's *Dialogues of the Dead* seems germane, as does Lord Lyttleton and Elizabeth Montague's more contemporary *Dialogues of the Dead* (1760). There is, too, *A New Dialogue of the Dead between Dean Swift and Henry Fielding*, attached to the comic miscellany titled *Tristram Shandy's Bon Mots* (1760). The caveat, I think, is that these inventive séances involve fictional versions of historical figures, not fictional versions of fictional figures, as in Yorick, but the basic trope rings true to Sterne's imaginative necromancy: that is, to resurrect the dead for a timely philosophical conversation. The history of ghost literature proper ought also to be mentioned, if considering sources. For example, Sterne keeps Dido's ghost close at hand, and also those shadows with whom Odysseus talks, as he searches for answers beyond the grave. Additionally, Dante's *Purgatory* haunts the *Journey*, or at least the thought of it, with special emphasis upon the parallel between Beatrice and Eliza. *Hamlet* must be noted as well, but in a new light. Specifically, we see that Sterne—through the *Journey*—poses a fascinating counterfactual question: How would the world change if Yorick's ghost, not the king's, exerted more influence? How would things be different? Rather than engaging in perpetual warfare, for instance, people might instead go to the theater, and from there to the bedroom. In fact, Sterne may have already answered this counterfactual query in the form of the "Fragment." Here, we discover the violent town of Abdera, a grim place, until—that is—the players perform Euripides's *Andromeda*, after which Perseus's love speech echoes through the neighborhoods: "in every street of Abdera, in every house, 'O Cupid! Cupid!'"[51] Such is Yorick's effect as well.

Fielding's ghost comedies also warrant mentioning, if considering the *Journey*'s source material, insofar as both contain a comic ghost. In *Tom Thumb*, a larger than normal Cow wanders into the street and swallows Tom whole, thus killing him, at which point his ghost returns to the stage, only to be killed a second time by Grizzle, in a scene now famous for making Swift laugh out loud.[52] In the *Tragedy*, Tom's father—Gaffney—appears as the ghost of record, mainly to parody the king's ghost from *Hamlet*, using mock-ominous language and making noises at midnight. When Arthur understandably threatens to kill him, Gaffney drolly replies, "I am a ghost, and I am already dead," which amuses those of us who remember Tom's double death in the play's previous incarnation.[53] Of course, these ghosts hardly qualify as sophisticated literary characters, unlike Yorick, but the idea behind them is sophisticated. Fielding satirically chides the moderns for doing so poorly with ghosts, if doing anything at all, a point clarified in one of *Tom*'s lengthy footnotes:

> Of all the Particulars in which the modern Stage falls short of the ancient, there is none so much to be lamented as the great Scarcity of Ghosts in the latter. Whence this proceeds, I will not presume to determine. Some are of opinion that the Moderns are unequal to that sublime Language which a Ghost ought to speak. One says ludicrously that Ghosts are out of Fashion; another, that they are properer for Comedy; forgetting, I suppose, that *Aristotle* hath told us that a Ghost is the Soul of Tragedy.[54]

A similar argument appears in *Tom Jones*, we might recall, when the narrator advises Christian writers on how to use the supernatural in their fiction without pandering to credulity or, worse yet, lapsing into bathos: "The only supernatural agents which can in any manner be allowed to us moderns are ghosts," but of such ghosts authors are "to be extremely sparing," lest they elicit "a horse-laugh in the reader."[55] All of this is to say that Fielding challenges his contemporaries to create ghostly intrigue, and Sterne answers this challenge, I believe, but in a manner more astonishing than the acolytes of the Enlightenment are prepared to accept, or even recognize. Three years earlier, Horace Walpole also answers the call in *The Castle of Otranto* (1764), replete with talking portraits, a skeleton ghost, and mediocre storytelling. If *The Castle* is the first full-blown gothic novel, and maybe it is, then the *Journey* is the first full-blown great gothic novel, and, unless I am mistaken, the first funny one, too, now to be set within a marvelous tradition of gothic comedy. Recent classics include *Young Frankenstein* and *Buffy the Vampire Slayer*—the series. In sum, if we accept Sterne's invitation to read Yorick as a ghost, we find ourselves in the company of strange bedfellows. Would Sterne have it any other way?

A second benefit of the ghost thesis is to provide an alternative explanation for the *Journey*'s dreamy style. At least since Virginia

Woolf's prologue, critics have rightly read Sterne's sentimental prose as a forerunner to the stream-of-consciousness writing exemplified by Proust, Woolf, Joyce, and many others, all of whom pursue a certain kind of psychological intimacy. As Woolf puts it, "Under the influence of this extraordinary style the [*Journey*] becomes semi-transparent. The usual ceremonies and conventions which keep reader and writer at arm's length disappear. We are as close to life as we can be."[56] And close to the afterlife as well, if Yorick is a ghost, which might also account for the *Journey*'s magical elements. Unlike the J. Alfred Prufrocks of the world, who tend toward disenchantment, Sterne's Yorick carries with him an almost otherworldly sensibility, a prophetic-nostalgic-sidereal-fairyland tint, for lack of a better phrase, made all the more peculiar by the incessant biblical allusions. Indeed, Yorick's eloquence resists easy classification; he oscillates between astral planes and linguistic registers, and exactly where he lands at any given moment is a matter of some debate. "The earth hath bubbles, as the water has," Banquo tells Macbeth, while he tries to explain the inexplicable presence and then absence of the weird sisters.[57] We are right to make a similar observation about Yorick's unexpected presence and then absence, with the corollary idea that his bubble is not of the demonic sort. Rather, he arrives through a different kind of conveyance entirely, something akin to the giant seashell upon which Sandro Botticelli delivers his *Venus*. And when Sterne delivers his Yorick out of the same ether and onto the earth, with a fanfare of cherubs in tow, we catch a brief glimpse of the world behind our world and realize, suddenly, that Yorick is not alive in the way we first thought. Or so goes the logic of the fleshy ghost argument. And, if true, then we cannot help but hear in Yorick's voice a paranormal timbre, which is to say that Sterne writes something other than modern stream-of-consciousness prose.

Finally, the ghost thesis connects Sterne more directly to the period's ample body of ghost philosophy, starting with Daniel Defoe's widely circulated *Essay on the History and Reality of Apparitions* (1727), which was reprinted in 1752 in under the title *A View of the Invisible World*. Here, Defoe recounts volumes of forgotten ghost lore, along with many contemporary stories, including one of an ethereal priest who returns from the grave to thwart an illicit liaison between a young woman and a wealthy but disreputable suitor.[58] And behind Defoe's work stands Joseph Glanvill's *Saddicismus Triumphatus* (1681), the early modern period's most important book on newly empirical supernaturalism. Glanvill, a Royal Society fellow, sets out to prove the existence of spirits, presenting evidence and providing a bevy of theological arguments, all aimed at blunting the threat of sadducism. By Glanvill's logic, and Defoe's, a disbelief in spirits inevitably leads to atheism. "Atheism is begun in Saducism," Glanvill observes, adding that those who do not believe in God "content themselves (for a fair step and introduction) to deny there are Spirits."[59] The *Journey* belongs to this same milieu of philosophical thinking, with the caveat that Sterne's work proves more entertaining and perhaps, too, more keenly aware of the challenges presented by a highly skeptical audience. Indeed, Sterne sets out to defend the Christian soul against the most refined of the atheistic cognoscenti, who have long-since rejected the ordinary modes of persuasion, for example, the sermon and the theological treatise. In the face of such a cultured materialism, how might he make an inroad? The funny answer is to tell a sentimental tale wherein a flirty ghost haunts France and, on occasion, attempts to explain ghosts to those who do not believe in them. For this irony alone, a ghost defending the existence of ghosts, the *Journey*'s ghost thesis recommends itself, but there is more to the story. Sterne understands the skeptic's fortifications against straightforward rhetoric, and so he takes a different route entirely, namely, a comic one through Protestant Purgatory. By doing so, he creates an unexpected religious argument, though to call it an "argument" might give the wrong impression. Sterne designs the

Journey as a spiritual–rhetorical atmosphere, not a syllogism, nor a set of presuppositions triumphantly asserted as conclusions, which too often is the modern evangelist's method of disputation. Rather, the *Journey* is best described as a site of supernatural energy, and within this field of energy we discover beautiful things, among them Sterne's love for the earnest materialists who do not want to believe, or no longer can. If the *Journey* persuades, then it persuades through this loving aura, for lack of a more precise description, and it does so to good effects, I think. A case in point: after reading Sterne's charmed rhetoric, Nietzsche described himself as "floating," which is not exactly to endorse the flying saints of medieval Christendom, but nor is it to speak harshly against Sterne's Christianity.[60] This is enough. Sterne upholds supernaturalism without alienating adventuresome atheists, who, in the twilight moments between waking and dream consciousness, may find themselves inexplicably wondering if ghosts are real. And if ghosts, then what else?

"A young man who wishes to remain a sound atheist cannot be too careful of his reading," C.S. Lewis once quipped, and this in relation to himself as a young man.[61] He resolved to maintain his rote materialism at all cost, until—that is—he encountered the weird spiritual ambience in Romantic literature, at which point he reevaluated the cosmos. To the young skeptics who read the *Journey*, and to the old skeptics, for that matter, the same cautionary note applies. They cannot be too careful.

6

Ghost Rhetoric

In the previous chapter, we parsed evidence for the ghost thesis but said little about why Sterne sends Yorick's ghost to France. For what purpose, or purposes, does he show us Yorick's final theosis? Here, I will attempt to answer this question. Perhaps most importantly, Yorick finds himself on a domestic mission, the aim of which is to acknowledge that he is Tristram's father, though "acknowledge" is not the right word. He loves Tristram and wants to be understood, and to this end discloses how he and Mrs. Shandy momentarily fell in love, if we are to call it that. Like many other riddles, however, this one arrives only in the dream language of the Shandyverse; nothing about the paternity theme is straightforward, nor should we want it to be. "Satire" is another good answer to the question of why Yorick returns, insofar as Yorick's ghost playfully critiques various mortal misconceptions of the universe. In particular, or of most interest here, at least, are his sendups of splenic travel writing, grave historiography, and vain religion, all of which invite more scrutiny than Yorick has time to muster, but he has time enough to dent the dignity of the overly serious. Lastly, Yorick's ghost clearly returns to flirt with women and tell bawdy jokes. This is not in keeping with the usual canons of final theosis, of course, but in defense of Yorick, and in defense of Sterne, such high-spirited behavior brings welcomed mirth to an otherwise often-melancholic scene, that is, the act of dying in order to live life eternal. In short, there are worse ways to be a ghost. That Yorick returns for other reasons, too, I have no doubt, but these mentioned above provide good points of departure. They reveal how Sterne uses Yorick's ghost to move our spirits and make us laugh, with the deeper hope also that we might "love each other,—and the world, better than we do."[1] Such is Sterne's optimism about the power of literature to transform peoples' lives, which is as timely now as it ever was.

The Unfinished Business

First, to the unfinished business. Yorick's ghost speaks to Tristram in the *Journey*, though perhaps not as directly as he might have hoped. A reunion was not meant to be. Nevertheless, he advises Tristram to travel wisely and, as much as permissible, explains the rapport he shared with Mrs. Shandy long ago, before Tristram's "*ab Ovo*."[2] Yorick's aim in all of this is to express fatherly love, however belated that expression might be, however long overdue. Better late than never. And his aim is to be understood by his son, a normal desire shared by all caring fathers. For the sake of convenience, I start with the premise that Tristram is Yorick's son, which many critics take for granted at this point, but if an argument need be made, then Richard Macksey makes it in "Sterne Thoughts," as does Sterne himself through the heavy-handed clues in *Tristram Shandy*: Tristram's lanky form, Walter's puzzlement over who the duce he takes after, Mrs. Shandy's well-timed silences in volume 9, etcetera.[3] Sterne hides the paternity in plain sight. On the question of what it means for the *Journey*, however, the plainness quickly disappears into the ether.

Yorick's semi-veiled communiqué to Tristram begins in earnest when he decides to find a copy of *Hamlet*, after the old French officer makes a profound observation about travel. He, the officer, stresses the extent to which "mutual toleration" teaches "mutual love," which causes Yorick to think suddenly of Polonius's advice to Laertes, not as a favorable comparison but rather as a strong contrast.[4] The officer speaks in defense of empathy and fellow feeling toward the stranger, perhaps even to a sentimental fault; he is—one detects—the proverbial Good Samaritan. On the contrary, Polonius urges a kind of Machiavellian practicality, mostly through familiar dictums: accept criticism, reserve judgment, keep thoughts to oneself, avoid gaudy clothes, and so on. Not that we should fault Polonius for his caution: sometimes paranoia is good thinking, as the old adage goes. Nevertheless, an unhealthy proclivity toward machination governs Polonius's mindset, which he passes on to Laertes, while a sympathetic disposition governs the French officer's mindset, and—by extension—Yorick's. This sympathetic disposition is what Yorick wants to pass on to those who stand in for Laertes, including Eliza, the sentimental and inquisitive readers, Eugenius, at times, and, finally, Tristram, if there is to be an elegant parallelism with Polonius and Laertes, the father and son who function as foils. Essentially, then, Yorick advises Tristram in an effort to circumvent Polonius's influence, understanding Polonius to be the archetype for a particular kind of well-intentioned though misguided pundit.

And this is to say nothing, yet, of Polonius's most famous pronouncement: "To thine own self be true."[5] In a hurried crescendo, Polonius delivers the maxim to Laertes, adding that if Laertes is true to himself, then it logically follows, as night follows day, that he cannot "be false to any man."[6] The syllogism, of course, is nonsense, and is also—I suspect—the deeper philosophical reason for why Sterne interjects Yorick into the Polonius-and-Laertes scene, beyond his sensible desire to temper Polonius's unsentimental pragmatism. Yorick intervenes because he knows that self-truth is tricky business, trickier than Polonius's placard suggests. For example, Alexander of Pheres gleefully murdered people precisely because he was true to himself, as Sterne explains in the Elijah sermon; the tyrant behaved like a tyrant, until—that is—he saw Euripides's *Trojan Women* and wept, at which point his authentic shallowness gave way to something more substantial.[7] Sterne observes the same of King David, only it was the prophet Nathan, not Euripides, who punctured his balloon of self-truth.[8] The best advice for all such tyrants, or tyrants in the making, is certainly not to be true to themselves. Instead, they ought to be true to an admirable person, or, better yet, a righteous ideal, with the caveat that only then will they become the types of selves for whom Polonius's dictum proves viable.

But even if we set aside the problem of true villainy, other difficulties persist: What about the self-deceived, for instance, or the self-equivocated? Hawthorne's Reverend Dimmesdale demonstrates the latter: "No man, for any considerable period, can wear one face to himself, and another to the multitude, without finally getting bewildered as to which may be the true."[9] As for the self-deceived, Sterne gives us The Prodigal Son, who was true to his grandiose self when he purchased the mummies and peacocks, not comprehending the inevitable disaster to follow.[10] Indeed, in Sterne's version, the prodigal thought himself heroic, a bold entrepreneur who would prove his family wrong, only to be hoisted by his own petard. Saint Peter, too, illustrates the point, as Sterne suggests in another sermon, insofar as Peter presumed himself to be fearless until he denied Christ three times, forgetting that "complete self-confidence is not only a sin," as G.K. Chesterton once observed, "but also a weakness."[11] In sum, "to thine own self be true" presupposes a naïve model of personhood, which is Sterne's basic point. Not that we are in the dark about ourselves, but self-awareness fails to make us foolproof, especially given our Herculean abilities to hide truths from ourselves. Thus, Yorick's ghost returns to remind Tristram not to be true to himself, at least not in the way Polonius means it, but rather to be true to the God of the "great—great Sensorium," in whom authentic self-orientation proceeds, by the edicts of Yorick's Anglican theology, and Sterne's.[12]

Beyond advising Tristram and others on the deeper wells of self-awareness, contra Polonius and Laertes, Yorick also returns to confirm his role in Tristram's conception. Like many other confirmations in the Shandyverse, however, this one arrives through dream rhetoric and so requires a tolerance for the weirdly metonymical. The scene in question involves Yorick and the grisette, specifically when he takes her pulse in the glove shop. Here, we must recognize that Sterne alludes to *Hamlet*. Confronting Gertrude in her closet, Hamlet sees his father's ghost, but Gertrude does not, at which point she accuses him of madness. He retorts, "My pulse, as yours, doth temperately keep time, and makes as healthful music: it is not madness that I have utter'd."[13] Afterword, Hamlet urges Gertrude to confess her sins and repent, but she refuses, and so the tragedy continues to unfold. For our purposes, however, the pulse is the thing. Specifically, Hamlet presumes to know that his mother's pulse keeps temperate time, which it obviously does not, at least not always. Hamlet is wrong, just as Tristram is impressively wrong in the exact same way about Mrs. Shandy's pulse, and not coincidentally: "A temperate current of blood ran orderly through her veins in all months of the year."[14] But why does Sterne—in the *Journey*'s pulse scene—slyly allude to these earlier pulse episodes in *Hamlet* and *Tristram Shandy*, where sons misconstrue the natures of their mothers' pulses? The answer comes in the form of a circuitous deduction: through the grisette-and-pulse scenario, Yorick symbolically communicates to Tristram the idea that he seduced Mrs. Shandy by taking her pulse, and this in the presence of an inattentive husband. Furthermore, Yorick rightly anticipates that such a revelation will upset Tristram, who will then confront his mother, at which point Yorick (via the *Hamlet* allusion) teleports himself into Gertrude's closet, where the pulse confrontation between son and mother occurs. In this intricate dream metonym, Mrs. Shandy plays Gertrude, Tristram, Hamlet, and Yorick, the king's ghost: Act 5, Scene 3. And here is where the Shandean miracle occurs. Sterne rewrites *Hamlet*'s tragedy in the form of a comedy wherein the ghostly father, rather than advising the son to seek revenge, urges benevolence, much like we imagine Shakespeare's own Yorick would do, had he returned from the grave to comfort Prince Hamlet.[15] Moreover, by virtue of his presence in the closet as Hamlet's father, that is, as Tristram's father, Yorick reveals what Mrs. Shandy would not reveal (i.e., paternity), presumably hoping that this revelation might somehow mitigate Tristram's suffering. Maybe it does.

Of course, revelations can be thorny things, as Ambrose Bierce's playful definition suggests: "Revelation: A famous book in which St. John the Divine concealed all that he knew."[16] The *Journey*'s grisette-and-pulse revelation undoubtedly requires a sensitive method of exegesis, if all is to come out in the wash, something akin to the method applied by those slightly neurotic readers who deduced that Tristram's mother was not a papist—well before Tristram announced as much.[17] In the case of Yorick's opaque confession, however, a different kind of caveat is warranted: when the dead speak, they do so in the dream language available to them, which in this case (for whatever reason) constitutes a French glove shop, a curious grisette, and her inattentive husband. It will do. It must do, and on some subconscious level, the idiom will make perfect sense to Tristram. Through these strange images, Yorick's ghost says in death what he did not say in life, though he had certainly planned to say it all before he died, and in clearer terms than these. But death interrupted him, as it interrupts us all, and so we are left to fill in the missing pieces. The moral of the story, then, is that today—not tomorrow—we should express our love for those whom we love, and today we should make amends wherever possible. Perhaps, too, a second observation is warranted, given the content of Yorick's revelation: those who presume to know the nature of a woman's pulse often look foolish.

Ethereal Satire

In addition to finishing unfinished business, Yorick's ghost also returns to write satire. As Juvenal once observed, "it is difficult not to write satire."[18] Even in death, apparently. And many things fall under the purview of Yorick's gentle mockery, including Yorick himself, it must be stressed, in case anyone should confuse Sterne's protagonist with the Ghost of Christmas Past, or some other solemnity-prone moralizing spirit. Most obviously, however, Sterne—through Yorick—targets those splenic travelers who always seem to find the thorns, not the roses. High prices. Bad roads. Rain. "The Anthropophagi."[19] The Smelfunguses and Mundunguses of the world suffer from a particular type of active negativity, or what the demon Screwtape calls "the gluttony of delicacy," that is, the talent at all times to make a fuss.[20] The tea is never quite warm enough, or cool enough, or sweet enough; the Parthenon, not as dignified as one had hoped ("*'Tis nothing but a huge cockpit*"); the Venus de Medici—beautiful, but problems inescapably persist.[21] If they must, the splenic writers will do "penance" in "Heaven" for "all eternity," Yorick tells us, which is an exaggerated way of saying that they are not yet ready to be happy.[22] Until they are, we should expect nothing more from them than "miserable feelings," as they go from "Boulogne to Paris,—from Paris to Rome,—and so on," with no pleasant anecdotes to tell, no happy conversations, looking neither to the left nor the right, "lest Love or Pity should seduce [them] out of [the] road."[23] Yet in the middle of this righteous satire, Yorick prays for the splenics, that they might exhaust themselves in one last entropic wheeze somewhere out on the Elysian Field's horizon, where the lost sheep are found and the wounded, healed. And where Yorick, too, might put to rest his own melancholy. And behind him, Sterne, whose suffering similarly informs the *Journal*, "a Diary of the miserable feelings of a person separated from a Lady for whose Society he languish'd," emphasis—once again—on "miserable feelings."[24] For all of Yorick's indignation against the spleen, there is—underneath—a palpable spirit of empathy and consolation. Why this should be the case proves more difficult to articulate, except to say that Sterne detects in the splenic traveler's cynicism what he detects in his own sadness, and this is the conspicuous absence of Aphrodite.

The splenic experiences loneliness, most often self-imposed, wittingly or unwittingly, and then perpetuated by an acerbic disposition. But loneliness is loneliness nonetheless, and herein Yorick discovers a way to identify with such prickly travelers.

To allay sullenness, Sterne recommends a version of playfully sentimental travel, the governing mantra of which is Ecclesiastes 8:15: "Then I commended mirth, because a man hath no better thing under the sun than to eat, and to drink, and to be merry: for that shall abide with him of his labor the days of his life, which God giveth him under the sun." But underneath the *Journey*'s loving mirth we discover also love in the house of mourning and love confined.[25] To the latter belong the captive and the caged starling, two sides of the same coin, one tragic and one comic, both of which Abraham Lincoln had in mind when he quipped, "I am like the starling in Sterne's story, 'I can't get out.'"[26] A rich allusion uttered by a man of feeling who, mindful of grave danger, nevertheless used his wit to help the proverbial injured man on the roadside. They will know we are Christian travelers by our love, Christ tells us in John 13, and, in Matthew 22, he requires that we love our neighbors as ourselves. And when the Pharisees asked Christ who constituted the neighbor, Jesus did not answer straightforwardly but rather delivered the parable of the Good Samaritan, a sentimental traveler par excellence.[27] Yorick aspires to be the same, sometimes effectively, and sometimes not, but that he knows the difference is clear. "Did we but love each other" as the poor German "loved his ass," Yorick observes on the road to Nampont, then "'twould be something."[28] Here, he comforts the distraught pilgrim whose donkey died in mid-pilgrimage, but finds time also to restate Christ's second great commandment in the form of an indecorous pun (i.e., we are to love each other as we love our own asses).[29] Thus is the deeper wisdom of Sterne's counterproposal to the spleen: a generosity beyond the self disrupts acrimony and makes possible a happier mode of travel.

Much like the splenic travelers, the grave historians also find themselves impugned by Yorick's otherworldly satire. Indeed, nowhere does Sterne marshal the parson's ghostly charisma more effectively than in the critique of grave historiography, a practice that collapses under the weight of its own self-importance. Or so Yorick cautions, the purpose of which is to advance a simple but profound truth: Heaven's priorities are not Earth's. Paradise, we have reason to believe, cares more for the builders of great monuments than for the monuments themselves. Such is the first tenet of sentimental historiography; people matter more than things, which partly explains why Yorick pays little witness to the Louvre's façade, for example, but of chambermaids and unaccompanied madams there is no shortage. Indeed, he conceives of "every fair being as a temple, and would rather enter in, and see the original drawings and loose sketches hung up in it, than the Transfiguration of Raphael itself."[30] To imagine as much is to recall John 2:19, where Christ declares, "Destroy this temple, and in three days I will raise it," to which the temple priests incredulously respond: "It has taken forty-six years to build this temple, and you are going to raise it in three days?" God's understanding of temples is not theirs, however, and from God Yorick takes his cue. Thus, he neglects "to swell the catalogues" with descriptions of important "pictures" and "churches," the "Palace Royal," etcetera, but faithfully archives a monk's downward glance and a lady's worried countenance.[31] And there are more "looks and limbs" and "inflections," too many to count, and also the copious promises to "bring pardons from Rome" to every damsel in distress.[32] If nothing else, such details show that Yorick is not a distracted historian, as some have concluded, but rather an exceptionally attentive one. It is as though he takes too much to heart Lucian's famous dictum in *How to Write History*: "The historian's one task is to tell the thing as it happened."[33] Or to accept too readily Quintilian's potentially disastrous rule of thumb: "It is worse to summarize all than to give every detail."[34] And so we have details galore, though not of the sort that usually appear in officially stamped chronologies, which is precisely Sterne's point.

The *Journey*, then, is Yorick's historiography of the intimate moment, which may seem like no historiography at all. Ian Jack once observed that "the experiences which matter to a sentimental traveler are precisely of the sort which leaves no record in the history books."[35] The same might be said of the sentimental historian, paradoxically. Or so Yorick demonstrates, as do those from whom he draws inspiration. The grave Bevoriskius sets the pattern. In a not-so-grave moment, he "breaks off in the middle" of his "Commentary" on "the Generations from Adam" to observe copulating "sparrows upon the out-edge of his window," which is an obvious emblem of the *Journey*'s methodology writ large, once we poeticize the sparrows as indicative of every meaningful moment that gets lost in time, or finds itself buried under the historian's official talk of warfare and empire.[36] Yorick's sentimental historiography contains something, too, of Thomas Gray's "Elegy Written in a Country Churchyard," lamenting "the short and simple annals of the poor."[37] Of course, the annals are not as simple as Gray imagines, but the noble sentiment nonetheless holds, both in Gray's poem and in Sterne's attentiveness to those obscure characters who haunt the half-lit alleyways and forgotten fields that more conventional historians call "barren."[38] And, naturally, the quixotic informs Yorick's methodology throughout. Indeed, Cervantes's critique of conventional historiography functions as the backdrop against which the whole of the *Journey*'s historiographical subplot proceeds. As Sancho observes:

> If the historians would only say, "Such and such a knight finished such and such an adventure, but with the help of so and so, his squire, without which it would have been impossible for him to accomplish it;" but they write curtly, "Don Paralipomenon of

the Three Stars accomplished the adventure of the six monsters," without mentioning such a person as his squire, who was there all the time, just as if there was no such being.[39]

Yorick, on the contrary, confirms that many such beings exist, motley crews in front of whom protagonists inevitably stand. Yorick remembers the proverbial squires. And, finally, if a biblical model is to be invoked in defense of Yorick's historiographical mode, then all of the book of Ruth should be imagined, particularly as the seventy-two masters of the Septuagint order it in the Old Testament. A modest love story, Ruth arrives immediately after the grim chronicles of Joshua and Judges and, as such, functions as a counterstatement to the historian's preoccupation with warfare. That is, Ruth functions as a beautiful interlude, a moment of bliss in a world otherwise given over to violence, wherein we catch a brief glimpse of Christ's makeshift earthly origins: Ruth the Moabite, the third of the five women mentioned in Matthew's genealogy.

And if there are objects and places to be noted in the *Journey* by way of underpinning Yorick's sentimental historiography, then they are also of the sort that do not usually appear in national registries. "I guard this [snuff]box as I would the instrumental parts of my religion," Yorick declares, "to help my mind on to something better."[40] As holy as any sacred relic in any reliquary, Father Lorenzo's snuffbox functions as a monument in the realm of sentimental historiography, as does the small London apartment that Yorick and Eliza are to share, "just big enough to hold a Sopha," as described in the *Journal*.[41] Yorick deems it "the sweetest of Earthly tabernacles," which he "shall enter ten times a day" to give Eliza "testimonies" of his devotion.[42] To the trained eye of the grave historian, such apartments require no account whatsoever, nor do the world's snuffboxes, but for the sentimental historiographer, they are the mementos of life itself, made holy not by the levers of cultural power but rather by the personal feelings attached to them. They are the proverbial keepsakes in shoeboxes under beds, or the now-tattered quilts made with love by arthritic grandmothers. And they are the secret places, like the clearing by the river where Hector's mother did laundry when he was a boy, which Hector—in the *Iliad*—glimpses out of the corner of his eye as he runs for his life from Achilles.[43] For a moment, Hector and we find ourselves transported back to a truer reality than the realism of war (i.e., the realism of laundry). Indeed, the world is full of such places, quietly reminding us of the people who matter more than all of history's pomp and circumstance combined.

In her well-known preface to the *Journey*, Virginia Woolf addresses this same topic of Yorick's unconventional historiography, though she offers an alternative explanation for why he proceeds as he does:

> The Cathedral had always been a vast building in any book of travels and the man a little figure, properly diminutive, by its side. But Sterne was quite capable of omitting the Cathedral altogether. A girl with a green satin purse might be much more important than Notre-Dame. For there is, he seems to hint, no universal scale of values.[44]

That Sterne downplays the Cathedral is undoubtedly true, and Woolf rightly detects as well that he has a philosophical reason for doing so, but her intimation that Sterne challenges a universal scale of values is wide of the mark, if by this she means that Sterne questions God's providential role in history. Sterne certainly undercuts the grave historiographer's typical values, to our delight and to Woolf's, but he does not leave the matter there, languishing in a kind of solipsistic subjectivity. Rather, through the precepts of Christian sentimentalism, Sterne reorients our value system, privileging *Imago Dei* and all that accompanies the idea. Once we understand his religious project, that is, to insist on the importance of people more than the importance of things, then we naturally prefer an interesting woman and her satin purse to the Cathedral's stony visage. And how much truer, still, if we find ourselves talking in euphemisms and double entendres?

In sum, Yorick's ghost has little patience with grave historiography. If possible, he has even less patience with vain theology, another of his important satirical targets. Indeed, Yorick seems actively unconcerned about the finer points of doctrine, as is perhaps most clearly demonstrated in "The Grace." Here, a peasant family shows Yorick hospitality by inviting him to dinner, after which they dance, sing, and laugh, in a scene that brings to mind Breughel's *Peasant Dance*, for example, or Tristram and Nanette's earlier dance on the French countryside.[45] And as Yorick watches the family's "jollity," he detects an ontological shift in the atmosphere, where the dance becomes worship: "I fancied I could distinguish an elevation of spirit different from that which is the cause or the effect of simple jollity. In a word, I thought I beheld *Religion* mixing in the dance."[46] Because he had spent too much time in Paris with the cosmopolitans, Yorick initially dismisses his spiritual intuition as an "illusion," until the family's old patriarch confirms it, suggesting that "a cheerful and contented mind was the best sort of thanks to heaven that an illiterate peasant could pay."[47] "Or a learned prelate," Yorick quickly adds, wholeheartedly welcoming the sentiment.[48] And in this welcoming of the sentiment, Sterne once again antagonizes the period's gloomy religionists, who will undoubtedly observe that neither Yorick nor the peasants have properly committed themselves to a particular atonement theory, a suitable Christology, a fittingly restrictive philosophy of Hell, and so forth, never mind the matter of communion, the one thing taken literally by the Catholics, as the Protestants complain. The Lilliputians and Blefuscudians will also have opinions and will certainly press Yorick and the peasants on which end of the egg they prefer.[49] But Sterne has another plan entirely, and this is to demonstrate through Yorick's spirit the simple and enduring disposition of the wise Christian. "Christianity," Yorick sermonizes elsewhere, "when rightly explained and practiced, is all meekness and candor, and love and courtesy."[50] Such is the theme of the "Grace" chapter, where Sterne quietly replaces the systematic theologian's cold machinery with warm banter and country folk dancing, two of the *Journey*'s best emblems of Heaven on earth, along with good wine and good sex. On the divine import of smokeless tobacco, however, we have reason to be dubious.

Yet vain religion will not be so easily vanquished, nor does Sterne have delusions of grandeur to such an end. Rather, he simply reproves those who would speak haughtily on God's behalf. This includes Yorick, instructively, whose first encounter with Father Lorenzo is a dreadful affair. The unsuspecting Franciscan solicits money for widows and children, in the spirit of James 1:27. A simple "no" seems beyond Yorick's capacity, and so he meets Lorenzo's request with scorn, the tone of which alone sends the monk into a graceful retreat. Lorenzo politely bows and gives a cordial "wave with his head," as if to say "no doubt there is misery enough in every corner of the world."[51] But Yorick, not ready to lose his audience, grabs Lorenzo's sleeve and thus continues with a grave admonition against ignorance and sloth, punctuated finally by an unwarranted crescendo: "For the love of God."[52] The phrase proves wholly ironic, of course, insofar as Yorick demonstrates the opposite of God's love in this awkward scene, which elicits "a hectic of a moment" across Lorenzo's face.[53] What we see, then, is a practitioner of true religion juxtaposed against a pretended religionist, a Pharisee who loves to hear the sound of his own voice more so than the sound of truth, in this case played temporarily by Yorick. The caveat, I think, is that most of us have played this role at one time or another. We are therefore relieved that Yorick's heart smites him in the next scene, confirming that he has not lost his moral compass, despite evidence to the contrary. "I have behaved very ill," he declares, and so resolves to "learn better manners."[54] And in this resolution, we discover the first of the *Journey*'s several theotic moments, where an imperfect priest exorcises negative energy from his soul, doing so through a combination of introspection and divine grace, not necessarily in that order, and certainly not equally weighted. The grace is the thing. Nor do we presume that Yorick has conquered his bad tendencies, just as we do not presume the same for ourselves, but we know that he wants to find a happier mode of travel, and in this desire there is hope. Put differently, Yorick confirms that his sermon on self-examination was not delivered in vain, with special emphasis on the best adage from it: "If a man is not sincerely inclined to reform his faults, 'tis not likely he should be inclined to see them."[55]

This first encounter with Lorenzo has a second positive effect as well, and this is to produce more evidence for the ghost thesis, if more evidence is needed. Yorick tells us that Lorenzo's countenance "look'd as if it look'd at something beyond this world," a remark that invites our speculation.[56] Maybe Lorenzo appeared as such because he did see something beyond this world, namely, otherworldly Yorick. That is, in his mind's eye, Lorenzo may have remotely viewed Yorick's grave prior to that beautiful scene where Yorick sits at Lorenzo's tombstone, snuffbox in hand, and openly weeps.[57] If so, if Lorenzo knew that Yorick was a ghost from the start, then how would we expect the good Franciscan to behave? The answer, I think, is that we would expect him to behave just as he does, an empathetic monk who extends and receives charity without judgment, whether involved with angels, prostitutes, or a ghost in the shape of a traveling priest. All such figures are welcomed at Lorenzo's table. "Be not forgetful to entertain strangers," Paul instructs in Hebrews 13:2, "for thereby some have entertained angels," and perhaps, too, fleshy ghosts.

Yorick, then, reprimands overly insistent religionists in the *Journey*, but not in an effort to ruin them. Rather, he sets out only to reform attitudes, starting most obviously with his own. The extent to which he succeeds is the extent to which he demonstrates love, the absence of which turns all of Christendom's confessions into "tinkling cymbals."[58] Put differently, Yorick models a better mode of being, a sentimental disposition that—by virtue of its very existence—sardonically undercuts the grave Goodman Browns of the world, who do as duty what happier souls do without thinking of it. Thus, Gardiner Stout is exactly right to describe Sterne's *Journey* as "a comic *Pilgrim's Progress* for the man of feeling," with the caveat that Sterne means no real harm.[59] Yorick's theosis is Yorick's, and if we see ourselves in his struggles, then all the better. And as for the puritanical travelers, Sterne—in his neighborliness—would have us remember Bunyan's earnest pilgrims in their best moments, well dressed and smiling, safe from the mount dooms of the imagination. Of course, we might be tempted to wonder if the hard-faced puritans will extend the same courtesy to Sterne, but it makes no difference: he blesses them regardless.

Conclusion

In this chapter's introduction, I postulated that Yorick's ghost returns to flirt with women, which is not exactly the correct way to characterize his motives. He returns to complete unfinished business and to deliver always-timely satire. Along the way, predictably, he also involves himself with various women, some scenarios more innocent than others. Such behavior confirms that Yorick is who he says he is, not a tepid doppelganger, but this clarity does little to tell us why he so incessantly philanders. How are we to understand Yorick's numerous liaisons, especially in light of his final theosis? What does Sterne hope to teach us?

There are two things to observe, I think, if aiming to comprehend the deeper rationale for Yorick's promiscuity, which in this case is a biblical rationale. The first is to notice a striking parallel between Yorick and Eliza, on the one hand, and Gomer and Hosea, on the other. Underneath both is the story of Israel's infidelity toward God, writ large across the whole of the Hebrew Bible. That is, Sterne gives us a straightforward allegory, and if it seems old-fashioned, or somehow strained, then consider his manifold references to Old Testament iconography: the sheep, the shepherds, the myrtles, the women who wail in the dessert. We find ourselves on the road "from Dan to Beersheba," often at midnight and in the marketplace, where Hosea pursued the prostitute Gomer and there, among the miniature golden calves, in the ancient world's Moulin Rouge, awkwardly declared his undying love for her.[60] The bad news, obviously, is that Yorick bears an unmistakable resemblance to Gomer, though in his case beset not by drunken male suitors but rather by aging coquettes and connoisseurs of the sort who frequent urbane salons. Not all is lost, however, despite the fact that Yorick succumbs to temptation, and this more than once. There is hope because Eliza proves true. In Sterne's mythic imagination, she functions as a metonym for the God who pursues us all, even into the grave.[61] Even past death, where we discover Yorick in a cramped hotel room with a Piedmontese lady and her chambermaid. Here, on the brink between this world and the next, in death's dream kingdom, Eliza also finds Yorick, at which point she declares her undying love. And he, the weary pilgrim, the lacerated lamb, hears her voice in the darkness and suddenly ejaculates "O, my God!," in what Elizabeth Kraft rightly describes as the *Journey*'s "Pentecostal moment."[62] Unsurprisingly, the Piedmontese lady and her chambermaid describe it otherwise. Nonetheless, the basic point holds: Eliza and Yorick function as an allegorical variation upon the troubled bond between God and Israel, with the caveat that God remains faithful, always, despite the wanderings of the devotees.

My second observation about Yorick's promiscuity relates to the first and, in fact, might precede it. This is to notice that Yorick cannot save himself. Indeed, it is worse than that. He must be saved from himself, as is perhaps most dramatically evidenced by his plan to see Madame de L— in Brussels. Soon after he declares his eternal fidelity to Eliza, and while he wears Eliza's picture around his neck, Yorick encounters the beautiful Madame and so begins immediately to daydream of their adventures together. But how might he rendezvous with the lady in Brussels and, at the same time, maintain his eternal allegiance to Eliza? This is the dilemma, and Yorick is certainly not the first man to pose it, nor the last. After some thought, and in a rhetorical–matrimonial maneuver worthy of the great Laputian philosophers, Yorick concludes that if he is to follow Madame de L— to Belgium, which he very badly wants to do, then he must bring Eliza with him: "I would not travel to Brussels," Yorick resolves, "unless Eliza went along with me," because to leave her at home would be inappropriate, if not outright unethical.[63] Thus, Sterne playfully mocks Yorick's self-congratulatory reasoning process, or bed of justice, which delivers the ridiculous verdict that infidelity might somehow be mitigated if one's true love is in tow.[64] Moments later, of course, and by God's prevenient grace, Yorick returns to his senses and confesses that "in transports of this kind," that is, in daydreams about alluring women, "the heart, in spite of the understanding, will always say too much."[65] And say too much it does, which once more demonstrates the unreliability of the conscience, an important theme throughout the *Journey*.

But lest we judge Yorick's ghost too harshly for his machinations, here and elsewhere, Sterne would have us also take a self-inventory, the purpose of which is to discover our own culpability in the human condition. And if we fail to see ourselves in Yorick's nonsense, then we have not yet looked deliberately enough through our own Momus windows. To know as much is not to commend ourselves, however, but only to understand the first principle of Sterne's theological–rhetorical–satirical program: we must be able to laugh at our own foibles, if we are to perform any semblance of virtuous satire, per Christ's comic admonition in Matthew 7:5: "Thou hypocrite, first cast the beam out of thine own eye; and then shalt thou see clearly to take the mote out of thy brother's eye." Together, then, we confront

Yorick's monumental efforts to fool himself into thinking that his benevolence is always benevolent, and his goodness—always good. Simultaneously, we confront our own dubiousness as well, which is no small task. Thus, we share with Sterne's quixotic hero a moment of mutual recognition, a knowingness and a nod punctuated by empathetic laughter, God-willing, and perhaps also a brief homily of the sort Tristram ejaculates to Jenny near the end of volume 9: "Heaven have mercy upon us both."[66] Indeed, Heaven have mercy upon us all.

7

Why Sterne?

To begin his piece for *The Columbia History of the British Novel*, John Allen Stevenson asks, "Why read Sterne?"[1] Good answers follow, not least of which is Sterne's brilliant use of sources and spectacular disregard for convention. And the intimacy and empathy of it all; and the beauty. Foremost for Stevenson, however, is Sterne's humor, and this in light of the fact that most humor travels poorly through time. What one epoch finds amusing another often dismisses as wrong. The jokes no longer work. The cleverness gets lost in obscure references and ruins. And yet against such headwinds, Sterne's comedy persists. The centuries have left untouched the best of his wit, and we have reason to believe that he will be equally hilarious in 2068, on the 300th anniversary of his death. Time will tell.

In the meanwhile, my aim in these concluding remarks is to provide some additional and admittedly more idiosyncratic reasons as to why we ought to read Sterne. Of course, in the previous chapters I have already offered several reasons, some more universal than others. Sterne may help us to exorcise the Devil from our smartphones, for example, or the metaphorical Devil, for those who doubt Satan's real presence. Inquisitive readers, if they pursue Sterne, will certainly become more familiar with biblical verses upon which relatively few sermons have been delivered: Judah and the goat, Jacob and Leah in the tent, and so forth. Sterne provides moral instruction as well, though the world's busybodies think otherwise. And—if we allow it—he shows us how better "to play gracefully with ideas," to borrow Oscar Wilde's phrase, and to borrow as well a sentiment from 1 Peter 3:15, where the author enjoins Christians to approach religious conversations with "meekness and fear," as the King James translation has it.² The English Standard Version says, "gentleness and respect." Additionally, Sterne offers an inspiring vision of final theosis, suggesting—among other things—that God's mercy extends far beyond the grave as we ordinarily think of it. This is not to invent a Protestant Purgatory, exactly, but rather only to reimagine the manner in which one dies in order to embark upon the supernatural sentimental journey. These are all good reasons to read Sterne, but if they do not persuade, I have others as well. Here, then, are four additional reasons why we might venture into the Shandyverse.

We might read Sterne devotionally, which need not be practiced only by the religious. As the atheist philosopher Alain de Botton has said on more than one occasion, religion has too many good ideas in it to be left to the religious alone.³ Nietzsche, for instance, found himself devoted to Sterne, and so did those early free thinkers who read *Tristram Shandy* as if it were a sacrament. Perhaps much of the fan fiction that imitates Sterne should also be seen in light of the devotional impulse, and much of the scholarship upon him as well, which is not necessarily devoted to the man but rather to the world he envisions, where levity defeats violence and love conquers all.⁴ The overtly religious may also read Sterne in the devotional sense, hoping to strengthen a faith that has grown too brittle over the years, or too grave. For spiritual ailments such as these, is there a better medicine than *Tristram Shandy*? And who better than Sterne to preserve the heart's tenderness, especially when those nascent forms of stoicism threaten to take hold after a traumatic event, or a hard year—beset on every side with difficulties? To read Sterne devotionally is not to obscure the reality of profound suffering, which is a given, but rather to disrupt the temptation toward despair. In Sterne, the energy of wit intervenes, as does the energy of urgent prayer, not unlike that of Thomas More's in the tower, when he prayed for good humor: "Grant me, O Lord, a sense of good humor" and a soul that "does not frighten easily at the sight of evil."⁵

Second, we might read Sterne in order to safeguard his Christian wisdom against a particular kind of historicist lore that inevitably develops around Christian writers, especially on the topic of theological relevance. Two examples come immediately to mind. Consider—first—Tim Parnell's argument that Sterne's Christian sentimentalism is all but lost to us now, remote at best and, at worst, inaccessible:

> No small part of what makes Sterne's sentimentalism "unreadable" for twentieth-century readers is that its theological underpinnings are almost entirely lost to us. While we can recover, from eighteenth-century sermons, part of the religious context that gave it meaning we can never, perhaps, reconstruct the belief that made it sincere.[6]

In defense of Parnell, relatively few Christians do seem to read Sterne, and fewer still discuss him in public forums and from an overtly Christian perspective. One can therefore understand why he concludes that Christians are no longer available to make sincere those beliefs put forward in *Tristram* and the *Journey*. At heart, however, the argument is a hasty generalization, insofar as I am evidence to the contrary, and there are others like me. Of course, one need not be a sentimental Christian to question Parnell's thesis, but more drama accompanies the argument when a Christian reader observes that Christians still read Sterne, and quote him in church peristyles, often to good effect.[7] There is also a broader point to be made, here, about the limits of historical thinking. If Sterne's sentiments are inaccessible, then how much more inaccessible is the parable of The Prodigal Son, for example, or the parable of the Good Samaritan? Or of all the ancient wisdom? What is to prevent us from dismissing Christ in total, who—as Melvyn New observes—is "the model of 'the man of feeling'" in eighteenth-century thought?[8] Put differently, and from an openly religious point of view, the deepest sentimental truths in life surpass any given historical context; in fact, I think it best to say that such truths, in Sterne and others, are not solely historical phenomena.

As a second example of historicist lore, take Richard Lanham's 1973 claim about *Tristram* and sexuality: "If we come to the day when sexuality is as public as eating, then *Tristram Shandy* will be as dead as *Eupheus*."[9] Some might argue that we have come to that day, or have come close enough to test the veracity of Lanham's hypothesis, and, if tested, it would surely fail. That we live in an age of public sexuality who would doubt? And yet Sterne is as popular as ever, and as relevant. But maybe Lanham has in mind an even more drastic version of public sexuality, not that such a version would change the argument. Fundamentally, he still must presume that *Tristram* is about sex in a rather simplistic way, and about very little else. Ergo, to demystify the sexual act is to antiquate Sterne. Yet I cannot help but think that *Tristram* would be all the more interesting in such a counterfactual world, mainly on the ground that Sterne delivers to us an entirely different kind of conversation than what Lanham imagines. *Tristram* has less to do with sex itself, in other words, and much more to do with sex and God, and death, and sin, and so forth. The list goes on for some time, but the idea—I hope—is clear: Sterne's theological-rhetorical orientation protects *Tristram* from hobbyhorsical efforts to circumscribe it historically. Or, put differently, Sterne's satires exceed their place and time, and—properly speaking—every particular place and time. They are, in a word, transcendent.

Third, and on a different note entirely, we might read Sterne in order better to appreciate C.S. Lewis's autobiography, *Surprised by Joy* (1955). Near the crux of any person's autobiography is their rapport with their parents, or their absent parents—or however the issue develops. It is a question of origin. And on that question, Lewis requires of his readers more than a passing knowledge of *Tristram Shandy*. Over the course of several amusing paragraphs, Lewis compares his father to Walter, while he plays the role of Tristram, in what amounts to a knowing reflection upon family life. He begins the scene as follows:

> My father—but these words, at the head of a paragraph, will carry the reader's mind inevitably to *Tristram Shandy*. On second thoughts I am content that they should. It is only in a Shandean spirit that my matter can be approached. I have to describe something as odd and whimsical as ever entered the brain of Sterne; and if I could, I would gladly lead you to the same affection for my father as you have for Tristram's. And now for the thing itself.[10]

Lewis proceeds accordingly, recounting his father's many eccentricities. He "was no fool," but at the same time "had—when seated in his own arm chair after a heavy midday dinner on an August afternoon with all the windows shut—more power of confusing an issue or taking up a fact wrongly than any man [ever] known."[11] For instance, "tell him that a boy called Churchwood had caught a field mouse and kept it as a pet, and a year, or ten years later, he would ask, 'Did you ever hear what became of poor Chickweed who was so afraid of the rats?'"[12] And besides the comedy of errors there were "the sheer non sequiturs," as when—for example—Albert Lewis doubted that Shakespeare used "Italian calligraphy" in the spelling of his name.[13] This is in good fun, obviously, and written with an enthusiasm for the Shandyverse, but Lewis has a second and unexpected purpose in mind as well: to needle his Cambridge colleague Frank Leavis, the man who excluded Sterne from *The Great Tradition* (1948). Specifically, infamously, Leavis dismissed *Tristram Shandy* as "irresponsible (and nasty) trifling."[14] Adding insult to injury, he did so in a footnote, which is probably the most quoted footnote in modern literary criticism. Nor was Leavis an admirer of Lewis, which brings us fully to the present connection. Many critics know that he disliked Lewis, but the American essayist Keith Mano most clearly confirmed the extent of the disapproval in an anecdote from his Cambridge days. Upon Lewis's death, Mano remembered this announcement from Leavis to his literature class: "C. S. Lewis is dead. They said in the *Times* that we will miss him. We will not. We will not."[15] Here, then, is the obscure reason why Lewis makes such a show of *Tristram Shandy* in his autobiography, published seven years after *The Great Tradition*: that is, to reject wholeheartedly Leavis's grave literary criticism. The forces of empire would have it that the emperor's clothes are real and the child imaginary. The forces of literary empire would have it the same, or at least those forces marshalled by Leavis and his acolytes. In *Surprised by Joy*, Lewis playfully suggests the alternative.

Finally, lastly, Sterne will help us not to take ourselves too seriously, which is easier said than done, especially when hot chestnuts fall into our pants, or thorns pierce our sides. Of course, there is a time for seriousness, as Yorick emphasizes, but never a time for the affectation of gravity in the service of Christian apologetics, which inevitably leads to that "mysterious carriage of the body to cover the defects of the mind."[16] And Sterne practiced what he preached, or, in other words, he took himself lightly. Perhaps he did this too well, his critics might object, but they object only out of distress. They have not yet envisioned that large rich plain at the end of time, where even those who have lost too much in this life will sing and dance for joy. And families will dance together with cheerful and contented minds. And Nanette will be there, too, with her self-taught politeness and "*Viva la joia!*" in her eyes.[17] Sterne knew what his solemn critics did not: the long arc of history bends toward mirth.

Notes

Chapter 1

1. John Paul II, *Theology of the Body* (Rome: Libreria Editrice Vaticana, 2005), 158–62.
2. John Kaltner, Steven McKenzie, and Joel Kilpatrick, *The Uncensored Bible: The Bawdy and Naughty Bits of the Good Book* (New York: HarperOne, 2008), 3. The Hebrew word translated as "rib,"—"tsela"— does not mean rib, exactly, but rather describes a hill's protruding side in 2 Samuel 2:16 and, more pertinently, the Ark of the Covenant's protruding handle in Exodus 25:12, giving new urgency to Epictetus's memorable dictum: everything has two handles—beware not to grab the wrong one.
3. Sterne, *A Sentimental Journey*, 1.72. See also Genesis 2:23 and *Tristram Shandy*, 1.21.78. Unless otherwise stipulated, references to Sterne are from *The Florida Edition*, 1978–2009.
4. On Isaiah 3:17, see Elon Gilad, "How the Prophet Isaiah Gave Hebrew Its Word for Vagina," *Haaretz* (September 1, 2015): Haaretz.com. On Jezebel's "palms," see Kaltner, McKenzie, and Kilpatrick, *The Uncensored Bible*, 103–4.
5. 2 Kings 9:33-35.
6. François Rabelais, *Gargantua and Pantagruel*, trans. Thomas Urquhart and Peter Motteux, ed. John Ozell (London, 1738), Book 4, Chapter 13.
7. Sterne, *Tristram Shandy*, 3.36.267.
8. Sterne, *Tristram Shandy*, 9.7.750. On Elisha and the Shunammite woman, see 2 Kings 4:8-17. On the Bible's lady wrestler, see Lyle Eslinger, "The Case of an Immodest Lady Wrestler in Deuteronomy 25: 11-12," *Vetus Testamentum* 31.3 (1981): 269–81.
9. Kaltner, McKenzie, and Kilpatrick, *The Uncensored Bible*, 100–6.
10. Joseph Cockfield, "Letter to the Reverend Weeden Butler," (1768), in *The Critical Heritage*, ed. Alan B. Howes (London: Routledge, 1974), 202–3.

11 John Wesley, from a journal entry (1772), in *The Critical Heritage*, 229.
12 Samuel Miller, *A Brief Retrospect of the Eighteenth Century* (1803), in *The Critical Heritage*, 325; Vicemus Knox, *Essays Moral and Literary* (1793), in *The Critical Heritage*, 254.
13 Ralph Griffiths, *Monthly Review* (1765), in *The Critical Heritage*, 163; D. Whyte, *The Fallacy of French Freedom, and the Dangerous Tendency in Sterne's Writings* (1799), in *The Critical Heritage*, 322.
14 William Wilberforce, *A Practical View of the Prevailing Religious System of Professed Christians, in the Higher and Middle Classes, Contrasted with Real Christianity* (1797), in *The Critical Heritage*, 301–2.
15 See the first sermon on Job (*Sermons*, 10: 99-100), Toby's critique of the Treaty of Utrecht (*Tristram Shandy*, 6.32.554), Trim's comment on the black maid (*Tristram Shandy*, 9.6.747–8), Yorick's comment on the starling (*Sentimental Journey*, 2.95–6), Yorick's profile of the captive (*Sentimental Journey*, 2.97–8), and Sterne's correspondence with Ignatius Sancho (*Letters*, 504–7).
16 Cash, *Sterne's Comedy of Moral Sentiments: The Ethical Dimension of the Journey* (Pittsburgh: Duquesne University Press, 1966), 11.
17 Friedrich Nietzsche, *Human All Too Human: A Book for Free Spirits*, 2nd ed., trans. R.J. Hollingdale, intro. Richard Schacht (Cambridge: Cambridge University Press, 1996), 238–9.
18 Hume, *An Enquiry Concerning the Principles of Morals*, ed. L.A. Selby-Bigge and P.H. Nidditch (Oxford: Oxford University Press, 1975), 270; Hume, "Letter to William Strahan," in *Letters of David Hume*, ed. J.Y.T. Greig (Oxford: Oxford University Press, 1932), 2:269: "The best book that has been writ by any English these thirty years (for Dr Franklyn is an American) is *Tristram Shandy*."
19 Jefferson, "Letter to Peter Carr" (August 10, 1787). On Lincoln's reference to *A Sentimental Journey*, see Doris Kearns Goodwin, *Team of Rivals: The Political Genius of Abraham Lincoln* (New York: Simon and Schuster, 2005), 488.
20 *Letters of Virginia Woolf: 1923–1928*, ed. Nigel Nicolson (New York: Harcourt Brace Jovanovich, 1975), 457. Woolf adds, "I was really shocked. A corpse would seem more credible to me than he is. I mean,

there's something obscene in a living person sitting by the fire and believing in God" (457).
21   Read suggests that Sterne "explicitly" reveals "his approach to life" in his sermons, while implicitly revealing the same "in his fictions" (*Essays in Criticism* [Freeport, NY: Books for Libraries, 1967], 134).
22   Sterne, Preface to the "Abuses of Conscience," *Sermons*, 27.255. See Cash, *Sterne's Comedy*; Melvyn New, *Laurence Sterne as Satirist* (Gainesville: University of Florida Press, 1969); Stephen Prickett, *The Romantic Appropriation of the Bible* (Cambridge: Cambridge University Press, 1996); Elizabeth Kraft, *Laurence Sterne Revisited* (London: Twayne, 1996).
23   Oscar Wilde, *The Importance of Being Earnest and Other Plays*, ed. Peter Raby (Oxford: Oxford University Press, 1995), 228.
24   Sterne, *Tristram Shandy*, 9.4.744; Thomas More, *Dialogue of Comfort against Tribulation* (1553), in *The Complete Works of Thomas More*, Volume 12, ed. Louis L. Martz and Frank Manley (New Haven, CT: Yale University Press, 1976), 155.
25   1 Peter 4:6.
26   Yogi Berra, *The Yogi Book* (New York: Workman Publishing Company, 2010), 13.
27   C.S. Lewis, *The Screwtape Letters* (New York: HarperOne, 2015), 54.
28   When asked about the source of *Tristram Shandy*'s original style, Sterne replied, "the daily reading of the Old and New Testaments" (Extract from Dominique Joseph Garat, *Mémoires historiques sur la vie de M. Suard* [1820], in *The Critical Heritage*, 414).
29   James Boswell, *Life of Johnson*, ed. R.W. Chapman, rev. J.D. Fleeman (Oxford: Oxford University Press, 1970), 696.
30   Ralph Wood, *Flannery O'Connor and the Christ-Haunted South* (Grand Rapids, MI: Eerdmans, 2004), 160.

Chapter 2

1   Sterne, *Tristram Shandy*, 1.19.62.
2   Sterne, *Tristram Shandy*, 9.22.777, 8.28.712.

3 Sterne, *Tristram Shandy*, 3.31.258, 6.2.494.
4 Anonymous, "Attack on Sterne and the Methodists" (1760), in *The Critical Heritage*: "The profane history of *Tristram Shandy* is as it were anti-gospel, and seems to have been penned by the hand of Antichrist himself" (100).
5 Sterne, *Tristram Shandy*, 5.26.457, 8.2.657, 1.8.13.
6 See W.G. Day, "*Tristram Shandy*: Locke May Not Be the Key," in *Laurence Sterne: Riddles and Mysteries*, ed. Valerie Myer (New York: Barnes and Noble, 1984), 75–83. See also Paul Davies, "The Line between Sterne's Novel and Locke's Essay," *Textual Practice* 31.2 (2017): 247–64; Arthur H. Cash, "The Lockean Psychology of *Tristram Shandy*," *English Literary History* 22.2 (1955): 125–35.
7 Sterne, *Tristram Shandy*, 4.20.356.
8 Sterne, *Tristram Shandy*, 7.25.614.
9 Coleridge, "Sterne," *The Literary Remains of Samuel Taylor Coleridge*, ed. Henry Nelson Coleridge (London: Pickering, 1836), 1:141.
10 Sterne, *Tristram Shandy*, 9.4.744.
11 Cited in Lewis, *The Screwtape Letters*, viii.
12 See Thomas Keymer, *Sterne, the Moderns, and the Novel* (Oxford: Oxford University Press, 2002). See also Tim Parnell, "Sterne's Fiction and the Mid-Century Novel," in *The Oxford Handbook of the Eighteenth-Century Novel*, ed. J.A. Downie (Oxford University Press, 2016), 264–81; Robert Folkenflik, "*Tristram Shandy* and Eighteenth-Century Narrative," in *The Cambridge Companion to Laurence Sterne*, ed. Thomas Keymer (Cambridge: Cambridge University Press, 2009), 49–63.
13 Warburton, "Reply to Sterne" (1760), in *The Critical Heritage*, 88.
14 Cited in Jane Shaw, *Miracles in Enlightenment England* (New Haven, CT: Yale University Press, 2006), 28. In 1969, the Anglican Church repealed canon 72.
15 See Francis Young, *A History of Anglican Exorcism: Deliverance and Demonology in Church Ritual* (London: I.B. Tauris, 2018); Brian Levack, *Possession and Exorcism in the Christian West* (New Haven, CT: Yale University Press, 2013); Moche Sluhovsky, *Possession, Mysticism, and Discernment in Early Modern Catholicism* (Chicago, IL: University of Chicago Press, 2007).

16 Hobbes said, "That there were many Daemoniaques in the Primitive Church and few Madmen, and other such singular diseases, where as in these times we hear of, and see many Madmen, and few Daemoniaques, proceeds not from the change of Nature, but of names" (*Leviathan*, ed. C.B. MacPherson [London: Penguin, 1985], 114).
17 Boswell, *Private Papers of James Boswell*, cited in Keith Thomas, *The Ends of Life* (Oxford: Oxford University Press, 2009), 232.
18 See Paul Kléber Monod, *The Occult in the Age of Enlightenment* (New Haven, CT: Yale University Press, 2013).
19 Whiston, *An Account of the Daemoniacks, and of the Power of Casting Out Daemons* (London, 1737), 74. See Stephen Snobelen, "Isaac Newton and the Devil," in *Newton and Newtonianism: New Studies*, ed. James E. Force and Sarah Hutton (London: Kluwer, 2004), 179.
20 Browne, *Religio Medici* (London, 1642), 57.
21 Shakespeare, *Hamlet*, ed. Sylvan Barnet (New York: Signet Classic, 1998), 1.4.40.
22 G.K. Chesterton observed, "The believers in miracles accept them (rightly or wrongly) because they have evidence for them. The disbelievers in miracles deny them (rightly or wrongly) because they have a doctrine against them" (*Orthodoxy* [New York: Dover, 2004], 73).
23 Sterne, *Tristram Shandy*, 5.16.448.
24 Sterne, *Tristram Shandy*, 6.33.557.
25 Cited in Arthur Cash, *Laurence Sterne: The Later Years* (London: Methuen, 1986), 105–6. Cash translates Sterne's letter, which is written in Latin.
26 See Battestin, "Sterne among the Philosophes: Body and Soul in *A Sentimental Journey*," *Eighteenth-Century Fiction* 7.1 (1994): 17–36. See also Battestin, "*A Sentimental Journey*: Sterne's 'Work of Redemption,'" *Revue de la Société d'études anglo-américaines des XVIIe et XVIIIe siècles* 38 (1994): 189–204.
27 Sterne, *Sermons*, 4:268.
28 See also Luke 8:26-37.
29 Sterne, *Tristram Shandy*, 5.16.447. Elizabeth Kraft suggests that "Sterne's own narrative preference, of course, is to give in to the devils" (*Sterne Revisited*, 74). I would phrase it differently.

30 Sterne, *Tristram Shandy*, 3.11.212; John 12:31; Sterne, *Tristram Shandy*, 3.31.257.
31 Sterne, *Tristram Shandy*, 2.12.130–1.
32 Sterne, *Tristram Shandy*, 6.18.526.
33 "Beelzebub," an onomatopoetic name, literally translates as "Lord of the Flies," and in Christian terms is one of Hell's princes (e.g., see *Pilgrim's Progress*, *Paradise Lost*). See New, *Notes to Tristram Shandy*, 3:438.
34 Sterne, *Tristram Shandy*, 3.11.212.
35 See Pierre Batiffol, "Apocatastasis," in the *Catholic Encyclopedia* (New York: Robert Appleton Company, 1907). See also C.A. Patrides, "The Salvation of Satan," *Journal of the History of Ideas* 28.4 (1967): 467–78.
36 Kraft includes the scene in her chronology of important events in Tristram's life, one of three incidents listed for the twenty-year span between 1720 and 1740 (*Sterne Revisited*, 49).
37 Quoted in C.S. Lewis, "The Inner Ring," in *The Weight of Glory and Other Addresses* (New York: HarperOne, 1980), 143.
38 Sterne, *Tristram Shandy*, 6.8.511. See also Revelation 12:10.
39 Revelation 20:12: "And I saw the dead, small and great, stand before God; and the books were opened: and another book was opened, which is the book of life: and the dead were judged out of those things which were written in the books, according to their works." See also Psalm 51:9: "Hide thy face from my sins, and blot out all mine iniquities"; Acts 3:19: "Repent ye therefore, and be converted, that your sins may be blotted out, when the times of refreshing shall come from the presence of the Lord."
40 Sterne, *Tristram Shandy*, 9.8.754.
41 Sterne, *Sermons*, 4:407.
42 Revelation 20:10: "And the devil that deceived them was cast into the lake of fire and brimstone, where the beast and the false prophet are, and shall be tormented day and night for ever and ever"; Revelation 21:8: "But the fearful, and unbelieving, and the abominable, and murderers, and whoremongers, and sorcerers, and idolaters, and all liars, shall have their part in the lake which burneth with fire and brimstone: which is the second death"; Matthew 25:41: "Then shall he

say also unto them on the left hand, Depart from me, ye cursed, into everlasting fire, prepared for the devil and his angels."
43 Sterne, *Tristram Shandy*, 4.S.T.310–11.
44 Sterne, *Tristram Shandy*, 7.14.594.
45 E.M. Forster," *Aspects of the Novel* (New York, 1927), 164.
46 Cowper, "Letter to Joseph Hill" (1766), in *The Critical Heritage*, 173.
47 Cited in Debora Shuger, "Foundations of Sacred Rhetoric," in *Rhetorical Invention and Religious Inquiry*, ed. Walter Jost and Wendy Olmsted (New Haven, CT: Yale University Press, 2000), 61.
48 Sterne, *Tristram Shandy*, 3.36.268. See Jeffrey Burton Russell, *The Devil: Perceptions of Evil from Antiquity to Primitive Christianity* (Ithaca, NY: Cornell University Press, 1987), 247. The black page could be read as oblique commentary on 2 Corinthians 3:15-16, where faith in God lifts the Devil's dark veil and allows us to see clearly.
49 Sterne, *Tristram Shandy*, 5.38.568. On Sterne's description of Yorick's death as autobiographical, see New, *Notes to Tristram Shandy*, 3:73-4.
50 Sterne, *Tristram Shandy*, 3.36.268.
51 Scholars have taken as axiomatic the idea that the black page somberly memorializes Yorick. This interpretation has a long genealogy, as Peter de Voogd shows: "The 1779 Dublin edition of *Tristram Shandy* has placed the phrase 'Alas, poor Yorick!' in the black page, thus turning it into a perfect tombstone" (*"Tristram Shandy* as Aesthetic Object," in *Laurence Sterne's Tristram Shandy: A Casebook*, ed. Thomas Keymer [New York: Oxford University Press, 2006], 111). But Tristram calls the black page a veil, not a tombstone, not a memorial, and he borrows the dark-veil-of-allegory idea from Peter Anthony Motteux's preface to Rabelais's works (see *Notes to Tristram Shandy*, 3:269–70).
52 Hannah Roberts, "Spike Milligan's Gravestone Quip Is Nation's Favorite Epitaph." *Daily Mail*, May 17, 2012: online.
53 Joyce, *James Joyce: Two Decades of Criticism*, ed. Seon Givens (New York: Vanguard Press, 1948), 11–12.
54 Cross, *The Life and Times of Laurence Sterne*, 3rd ed. (New Haven, CT: Yale University Press, 1929), 147. For the image of Trim's swirl, see *Tristram Shandy*, 9.4.743.

55 Ferguson, *Reason and Religion* (London, 1675), 308.
56 Sterne, *Tristram Shandy*, 3.36.268, 7.31.629.
57 New, "Preface," *Notes to the Sermons*, xiii.
58 Sterne, *Tristram Shandy*, 3.19.225.
59 Burton, *Anatomy of Melancholy* (New York: New York Review of Books, 2001), 366.
60 Sterne, *Tristram Shandy*, 1.23.82. We know from the mottoes to volumes 5 and 6 that the charge of clerical hypocrisy rankled Sterne. The marbled page confronts this charge preemptively with a bit of Scripture aimed directly at the critics of his bawdry, whom Sterne saw as the real hypocrites.
61 Prior, *Literary Works of Matthew Prior*, ed. H. Bunker Wright and Monroe K. Spears (Oxford: Oxford University Press, 1959), 409.
62 Sterne, *Tristram Shandy*, 2.2.85.
63 de Voogd, "Sterne and Visual Culture," in *Cambridge Companion to Sterne*, 145.
64 Harries, "Sterne's Novels: Gathering Up the Fragments," *English Literary History* 49.1 (1982): 38.
65 Patrides, *The Grand Design of God: The Literary Form of the Christian View of History* (London: Routledge, 1972), 47.
66 Sterne, *Tristram Shandy*, 5.38.566.
67 Sterne, *Tristram Shandy*, 2.17.142–64, 4.25.375.
68 Chaucer's Wife of Bath understood Christ's admonition as opening the possibility of divorce and remarriage based on the stipulation in Matthew 5:31-32.
69 Sterne, *Sermons*, 4:16. Sterne alludes to Mark 9:25-26, where Christ casts out a demon from a boy: "When Jesus saw that the people came running together, he rebuked the foul spirit, saying unto him, I charge thee, come out of him, and enter no more into him. And the spirit cried, and rent him sore, and came out of him." See also Mark 16:9, where Christ casts seven devils out of Mary Magdalene.
70 Sterne, *Sermons*, 4:290.
71 Sterne, *Sermons*, 4.64.
72 New, *Notes on the Sermons*, xx.

Chapter 3

1. Fitzgerald, *The Life of Laurence Sterne*, 1864 (London: Downey and Co., 1896), I.164, 56.
2. Gray, "Letter to Thomas Warton" (1760), in *The Critical Heritage*, 89.
3. New, *Notes to the Sermons*, vii–viii.
4. New, *Notes to the Sermons*, 17. See also Tim Parnell, "The Sermons of Mr. Yorick," in *The Cambridge Companion to Laurence Sterne*, ed. Thomas Keymer (Cambridge: Cambridge University Press, 2009), 64–78.
5. Gerard, "Introduction," in *Divine Rhetoric: Essays on the Sermons of Laurence Sterne*, ed. Gerard (Newark: University of Delaware Press, 2010), 14.
6. Sterne, *A Sentimental Journey*, 116.
7. Sterne, *Letters*, 252.
8. See New, "Sterne, Warburton, and the Burden of Exuberant Wit," *Eighteenth-Century Studies* 15 (1982): 245–74.
9. Sterne, *Sermons*, 22: 210.
10. Genesis 27:11. One wonders if Rachel made a similar remark about herself contra Leah.
11. Arthur Cash, *Laurence Sterne*, 105–6.
12. On Sterne's sexual subtexts, see Frank Brady, "*Tristram Shandy*: Sexuality, Morality, and Sensibility," *Eighteenth-Century Studies* 4 (1970): 41–56. See also New, "A Note on Annotating *Tristram Shandy*," in *Laurence Sterne: Riddles and Mysteries*, 15–23.
13. Sterne, *Sermons*, 27:257.
14. Sterne, *Sermons*, 27:257.
15. Cash, *Sterne's Comedy of Moral Sentiments*, 104–5.
16. Pascal, *Pensées*, trans. A.J. Krailsheimer (New York: Penguin, 1995), 127.
17. Raymond Anselment explains that Elijah's jest was the "most documented illustration of divinely sanctioned ridicule" in the early modern period (*Marprelate, Milton, Marvell, Swift and the Decorum of Religious Ridicule* [Toronto: University of Toronto Press, 1979], 66). Sterne also refers to this taunt in "The Case of Elijah and the Widow of Zarephath" (*Sermons*, 5:46).

18 Sterne, *Sermons*, 27:258.
19 Sterne, *Sermons*, 25:242.
20 South, *Forty-Eight Sermons*, 3rd ed. (London, 1715), 3:433.
21 New, *Notes to the Sermons*, 273.
22 Swift, *Tale of a Tub and Other Works*, ed. Angus Ross and David Woolley (Oxford: Oxford University Press, 2008), 88.
23 Sterne, *Tristram Shandy*, 7.25.614.
24 Sterne, *Tristram Shandy*, 5.38.566.
25 Elizabeth Harries theorizes Sterne's "pathos of the unfinished" ("Sterne's Novels: Gathering Up the Fragments," 41). I am suggesting a comedy of the unfinished. On some of Sterne's other techniques for comic effect, see *Hilarion's Asse: Laurence Sterne and Humour*, ed. Anne Bandry-Scubbi and Peter de Voogd (Newcastle: Cambridge Scholars Press, 2013).
26 Sterne, *Sermons*, 18:167.
27 Sterne, *Sermons*, 18:167–8.
28 Cited in Vincent Fitzpatrick, *H.L. Mencken* (Macon: Mercer University Press, 2004), 37.
29 Cash, *Sterne's Comedy of Moral Sentiments*, 165.
30 Rose, *Monthly Review* 34 (1766), 215.
31 See, for example, Rabbi A.J. Rosenberg and Rabbi Reuven Hochberg's *The Book of Kings 1: A New Translation of the Text, Rashi and a Commentary Digest*: "Others explain that the woman demanded that Elijah receive her son, lest people interpret his death as a punishment for immoral acts that she committed with Elijah" (New York: The Judaica Press, 1988), 181–2.
32 Psalms 68:5 and 146:9 are also commonplace verses in matters of widows and orphans.
33 Sterne, *Sermons*, 26.251.
34 Wodehouse, *Right Ho, Jeeves* (London: Barrie & Jenkins, 1978), 46.
35 Sterne, *Sermons*, 20.193.
36 Sterne, *Tristram Shandy*, 7.43.651. In critiquing the grand tour, Sterne draws upon Bishop Hall's satirical invective *Quo Vadis? A Just Censure of Travel, as It Is Commonly Undertaken by the Gentlemen of Our Nation* (1617).

37 Sterne, *Sermons*, 23: 216–17.
38 Bierce, *The Unabridged Devil's Dictionary* (1911), ed. David Schultz and S.J. Joshi (Athens: University of Georgia Press, 2000), 35, 109.
39 Sterne, *The Letters of Laurence Sterne*, ed. Lewis P. Curtis (Oxford: Oxford University Press, 1935), 404.
40 Sterne, *Tristram Shandy*, 2.11.125.
41 Sterne, *Letters*, 134.
42 See Sterne's sermon on pride: "Survey yourselves, my dear Christians, a few moments in this light—behold a disobedient, ungrateful, intractable and disorderly set of creatures, going wrong seven times in a day" (24.232).
43 When Hawthorne, for example, described Sterne's sermons as "the best ever written," we might rightly wonder if his judgment falls on the sermons themselves or the sermons and their circumstances together (James Fields, *Yesterdays with Authors* [Boston, MA: J.R. Osgood, 1872], 62).
44 New, *Notes to the Sermons*, 1.
45 Franklin, "Letter to Richard Jackson" (1763), in *The Critical Heritage*, 17.
46 Ruffhead, *Monthly Review* (1760), in *The Critical Heritage*, 77–8.
47 New, "Sterne's Rabelaisian Fragment: A Text from the Holograph Manuscript," *PMLA* 87.5 (1972): 1089.
48 Gow, "A Brief Account of Sterne's Homiletic Piracy," *Divine Rhetoric*, 123–48. See also Gow, "Were Sterne's Sermons Novel?" *The Shandean* 24 (2013): 70–83.
49 Sterne, "Preface," *Sermons*, 2.
50 Kraft, *Sterne Revisited*, 27.
51 New, *Notes to the Sermons*, 2.
52 Eliot, *Selected Prose of T.S. Eliot*, ed. F. Kermode (London: Faber & Faber, 1975), 153; Burton, "Democritus to the Reader," *Anatomy of Melancholy*, 25.
53 Sterne, *Tristram Shandy*, 6.10.514.
54 Lansing vander Leyden Hammond, *Laurence Sterne's Sermons of Mr. Yorick* (New Haven, CT: Yale University Press, 1948).
55 New, *Notes to the Sermons*, xvi–xvii.
56 Excerpt from an anonymous review (1766), in *The Critical Heritage*, 171.
57 Jefferson, "Letter to Peter Carr," August 10, 1787.

Chapter 4

1. Sterne, *Tristram Shandy*, 9.25.782; Sterne, *Sentimental Journey*, 2.154.
2. As New and Day remark, "Perhaps no scene in eighteenth-century literature has been illustrated more than this meeting between Maria and Yorick" (*Notes to* A Sentimental Journey, 367). On illustrations of the Maria scenes, see W.B. Gerard, "Changing Views toward Sentimentality Reflected in Visualizations of Sterne's Maria, 1773–1888," *Studies in Eighteenth-Century Culture* 34 (2005): 197–269; Catherine Gordon, *British Paintings of Subjects from the English Novel, 1740–1870* (New York: Garland, 1988), 74–6.
3. Kraft, *Sterne Revisited*, 119.
4. Purton, *Dickens and the Sentimental Tradition* (London: Anthem Press, 2012), 38.
5. Keymer, "*A Sentimental Journey* and the Failure of Feeling," 90–1; McGlynn, "Sterne's Maria: Madness and Sentimentality," *Eighteenth-Century Life* 3 (1976): 39–43.
6. New and Day, *Notes to* A Sentimental Journey, 368–9; Dussinger, "Madness and Lust in the Age of Sensibility," in *Sensibility in Transformation*, ed. Syndy McMillen Conger (Rutherford, NJ: Fairleigh Dickinson University Press, 1990), 85–6.
7. *The Big Lebowski*, Universal Studios, 1998.
8. See Gerard, "Changing Views toward Sentimentality," 238, 243.
9. Calum Carmichael, "A Ceremonial Crux: Removing a Man's Sandal as a Female Gesture of Contempt," *Journal of Biblical Literature* 96.3 (1977): 321–36. See also Deuteronomy 25: 7-10.
10. Ruth 4:12.
11. Ruth 3: 10-11.
12. Genesis 19: 31-38.
13. Sterne, *Sermons*, 22.206.
14. Dominique-Joseph Garat, *Mémoires historiques sur le XVIIIe siècle et sur M.Suard* (1820), in *The Critical Heritage*, 414.
15. Keymer, "Marvell, Thomas Hollis, and Sterne's Maria: Parody in *A Sentimental Journey*," *The Shandean* 5 (1993): 9–31. See also Anna

Verestói, "The Presence of Pastoral in Sterne's Maria Scenes," *The Shandean* 20 (2009): 113–25.
16 Sterne, *Tristram Shandy*, 9.1.735–37; Song of Solomon 5: 4–5.
17 Sterne, *Tristram Shandy*, 9.24.784.
18 Gordon Williams, *A Dictionary of Sexual Language and Imagery in Shakespearean and Stuart Literature*, 3 vols. (New York: Athlone Press, 1994), 2.714.
19 Williams, *A Dictionary of Sexual Language*, 2.714.
20 Griffiths, *Monthly Review* 36 (London: R. Griffiths, 1767): 98–9.
21 Griffiths, *Monthly Review*, 98–9.
22 Holland, *The Beauties of Sterne* (London: C. Etherington, 1782), 92. On *The Beauties of Sterne*, see Mary Newbould, "Wit and Humour for the Heart of Sensibility: The Beauties of Fielding and Sterne," in *The Afterlives of Eighteenth-Century Fiction*, ed. Daniel Cook and Nicholas Seager (Cambridge: Cambridge University Press, 2015), 133–52.
23 Paul Franssen, "The Earl of Clonmell Reads Sterne," *The Shandean* 2 (1990): 170.
24 de Voogd, "Sterne and Visual Culture," 150–1.
25 Sterne, *Tristram Shandy*, 9.24.783.
26 Sterne, *Tristram Shandy*, 7.43.649–51. See also *The Oxford English Dictionary*, s.v. "goat": "a licentious man."
27 On the Maria scene as an advertisement for *A Sentimental Journey*, see Gardiner Stout, ed., *A Sentimental Journey* (Berkeley: University of California Press, 1967), 16; Rufus Putney, "The Evolution of *A Sentimental Journey*," *Philological Quarterly* 19 (1940): 364–7.
28 Sterne, *A Sentimental Journey*, 2.152.
29 Sterne, *A Sentimental Journey*, 2.152.
30 Genesis 38:9: "And Onan knew that the seed should not be his; and it came to pass, when he went in unto his brother's wife, that he spilled it on the ground, lest that he should give seed to his brother."
31 Sterne, *A Sentimental Journey*, 2.150, 1.59.
32 Sterne, *Tristram Shandy*, 7.24.782.
33 Sterne, *Tristram Shandy*, 7.24.781.

34 While searching for "sisterly kisses" that are more than what they seem, we might also recall that Abraham twice referred to Sarah—his wife—as his sister (Genesis 12:13, 20: 2). On kissing as a euphemism for copulation in the eighteenth century, see Joseph Pappa, *Carnal Reading* (Newark, NJ: University of Delaware Press, 2011), 95.
35 Ephram Chambers, *Cyclopaedia, or, An Universal Dictionary of Arts and Science*, 2 vols. (London: 1728), 1.163.
36 See *The Oxford English Dictionary*, s.v. "damsel": "App. a humorous allusion to 1 Kings i.1-4."
37 Sterne, *Tristram Shandy*, 9.24.784.
38 Purton, *Dickens and the Sentimental Tradition*, 38.
39 Hogarth, *Before* and *After*. Oil on canvas, 1730-1. Fitzwilliam Museum, Cambridge, UK.
40 *American Beauty*, DreamWorks, 1999.
41 Sterne, *A Sentimental Journey*, 2.152.
42 Sterne, *A Sentimental Journey*, 2.152.
43 Sterne, *A Sentimental Journey*, 2.154.
44 Sterne, *A Sentimental Journey*, 2.152.
45 Oscar Wilde, *The Picture of Dorian Gray*, in *The Major Works*, ed. Isobel Murray (New York: Oxford University Press, 1989), 61-2.
46 Auden, "Atlantis," in *Collected Poems*, ed. Edward Mendelson (New York: Penguin, 2007), 314.
47 Sterne, *A Sentimental Journey*, 2.152; Sterne, *Tristram Shandy*, 9.24.783.
48 Shakespeare, *The Comedy of Errors*, ed. Sylvan Barnet and Harry Levin (New York: Signet, 2002), 2.2.131-34.
49 Shakespeare, *The Comedy of Errors*, 2.2.137-45.
50 Shakespeare, *Macbeth*, ed. Sylvan Barnet (New York: Signet, 1998), 5.1.38.
51 Sterne, *A Sentimental Journey*, 2.152.
52 Sterne, *A Sentimental Journey*, 2.154.
53 McGlynn, "Sterne's Maria," 41.
54 The "poor man" in Nathan's allegory is Uriah, Bathsheba's husband, and David is the one who took his only lamb (i.e., Bathsheba); incensed by the injustice in Nathan's story, David orders the villain's immediate execution, only to discover that he is the villain in question.

55 Leviticus 18:23: "And you shall not lie with any animal and so make yourself unclean with it, neither shall any woman give herself to an animal to lie with it: it is perversion."
56 Knox, *Essays Moral and Literary* (1793), in *The Critical Heritage*, 254. Knox cites Ruth 1: 16-17.
57 Knox, *Essays Moral and Literary*, 254.
58 On Esdras, see Sterne, *A Sentimental Journey*, 1.23. On Mary Magdalen, see Steven Shankman, "The End of Laurence Sterne's *A Sentimental Journey* and the Resistance to Doctrine," *Religion & Literature* 29.3 (1997): 56.
59 Sterne, *A Sentimental Journey*, 2.150; Sterne, *Tristram Shandy*, 9.34.783. On Dido, see Kraft, *Sterne Revisited*, 117–19. For more on Maria, see Kraft, "Bohemian Sterne," in *Sterne, Tristram, Yorick: Tercentenary Essays on Laurence Sterne*, ed. Melvyn New, Peter de Voogd, and Judith Hawley (Newark, NJ: University of Delaware Press, 2015), 28; Brigitte Friant-Kessler, "*Tristram Shandy*'s Mirroring Images," *Bulletin de la Société d'Etudes Anglo-Américaines des XVIIe et XVIIIe Siècles* 63 (2006): 73–4.
60 Matthew 1:1-16. See also Ruth 4:12.
61 Keymer, "*A Sentimental Journey* and the Failure of Feeling," 91; Henry Fielding, *Joseph Andrews* and *Shamela*, ed. Douglas Brooks (Oxford: Oxford University Press, 1970), 322. See also New and Day, *Notes to* A Sentimental Journey, 368–9.
62 Sterne, *A Sentimental Journey*, 2.149.
63 Sterne, *Tristram Shandy*, 7.42.646. On the bawdy import of "et cetera," see Williams, *A Dictionary of Sexual Language and Imagery in Shakespearean and Stuart Literature*, 1.448–9. See also Keymer, "Introduction," in *Joseph Andrews and Shamela*, ed. Keymer (Oxford: Oxford University Press, 2008), xi–xii; Sheridan Baker, "Fielding: The Comic Reality of Fiction," in *The Eighteenth-Century English Novel*, ed. Harold Bloom (Philadelphia, PA: Chelsea House, 2004), 148; Eric Partridge, *Shakespeare's Bawdy* (New York: Routledge, 2001), 129–30.
64 Sterne, *Tristram Shandy*, 5.1.411. In *Yorick's Sentimental Journey Continued*, John Hall-Stevenson makes more explicit the sexual import of "Ave Maria" in a scene where a "lusty friar" and a "mademoiselle"

have a devotion together ([London: S. Bladon, 1769], 4.52–3). See also Warren Oakley, *Laurence Sterne, His Readers and the Art of Bodysnatching* (London: MHRA, 2010), 85.

65   Keymer shows that "Sylvio" likely refers to a character in Marvell's "Nymph complaining for the Death of Her Faun," but Sylvio might also—in a different register—slyly allude to Franciscus Sylvius, the father of iatrochemistry, a figure with whom Sterne would have been familiar.

66   Hebrews 13:18: "Pray for us: for we trust we have a good conscience, in all things willing to live honestly"; Sterne, *Sermons*, 27.255.

67   Sterne, *Sermons*, 20.190.

68   Hogarth, *A Harlot's Progress*. Engraving with etching, 1732, Royal Collection Trust, London, UK. For more on Hogarth, see Ronald Paulson, *Hogarth's Harlots: Sacred Parody in Enlightenment England* (Baltimore, MD: Johns Hopkins University Press, 2003), 83.

69   On Sterne's genius and eighteenth-century bawdry, see New, "Sterne's Bawdry: A Cautionary Tale," *Review of English Studies* 62 (2010): 80–9. See also Frank Brady, "*Tristram Shandy*: Sexuality, Morality, and Sensibility," 41–56.

70   Sterne, *A Sentimental Journey*, 2.159.

71   Shakespeare, *Much Ado about Nothing*, ed. Sylvan Barnet (New York: Signet, 1998), 2.3.243–55.

72   Shakespeare, *Much Ado about Nothing*, 1.1.49–50.

73   Lewis, *Mere Christianity* (New York: HarperOne, 2000), xii.

Chapter 5

1   Sterne, *Tristram Shandy*, 1.12.35.

2   Elizabeth Kraft, *Sterne Revisited*, 105.

3   Thomas Keymer, "*A Sentimental Journey* and the Failure of Feeling," 89; Sterne, *A Sentimental Journey and Other Writings*, ed. Ian Jack and Tim Parnell (Oxford: Oxford University Press, 2003), viii. See also Ian Campbell Ross, "'Alas, Poor Yorick!': Death and the Comic Novel,"

Oxford University Press Blog (March 18, 2018): blog.oup.com; Ross, *Laurence Sterne: A Life* (Oxford: Oxford University Press, 2001), 19; John Mullan, "The Life and Opinions of Laurence Sterne: The First Unapologetic Literary Celebrity," *The Guardian* (March 15, 2018): theguardian.com; Cash, *Sterne's Comedy*, 31.

4   John Stedmond, *The Comic Art of Laurence Sterne* (Toronto: University of Toronto Press, 1967), 160; Elizabeth Goodhue, "When Yorick Takes His Tea," *Journal of Early Modern Cultural Studies* 6.1 (2006): 51–2.

5   Martin Battestin called Sterne "the first philosophical novelist in English" ("*A Sentimental Journey*: Sterne's 'Work of Redemption,'" 192).

6   Sterne, *Sentimental Journey*, 1.76.

7   Sterne, *Tristram Shandy*, 1.12.35.

8   Sterne, *Tristram Shandy*, 2.17.167.

9   Mathew 5:27.

10 Virgil, *The Aeneid*, trans. A.S. Kline (London: Poetry in Translation, 2002), Book 6, Line 443; See also *The Aeneid*, trans. C. Day Lewis (Oxford: Oxford University Press, 1952), Book 6, line 443.

11 Sterne, *Bramine's Journal*, 178.

12 Sterne, *Bramine's Journal*, 200, 192. "By sentimental magic," Jonathan Lamb observes, "the jester is turned into the king's ghost and Eliza is turned into Hamlet" ("Sterne's System of Imitation," *The Modern Language Review* 76.4 [1981]: 809).

13 Sterne, *Tristram Shandy*, 4.1.302.

14 On occult philosophy in Sterne's era, see Paul Kléber Monod, *The Occult in the Age of Enlightenment*. On ghosts, see Sasha Handley, *Ghost Beliefs and Ghost Stories in Eighteenth-Century England* (London: Pickering & Chatto, 2007).

15 Sterne, *Letters*, 350.

16 Swift, *The Mechanical Operation of the Spirit*, in *A Tale of a Tub and Other Works*, 141.

17 Swift, *The Mechanical Operation of the Spirit*, 141.

18 Lewis, "The Weight of Glory," in *The Weight of Glory and Other Addresses*, 44.

19 Paul Noth, "I Always Figured Hell Would Be Less Ironic," *The New Yorker*, October 22, 2007. On Christian views of Heaven, see Colleen McDannell and Bernhard Lang, *Heaven: A History* (New Haven, CT: Yale University Press, 2001).
20 Sterne, *Letters*, 350.
21 Sterne, *Tristram Shandy*, 7.25.614.
22 Sterne, *Letters*, 351.
23 On John Dee and Edward Kelly, see Deborah Harkness, *John Dee's Conversations with Angels* (Cambridge: Cambridge University Press, 1999), 19–23.
24 Sterne, *Bramine's Journal*, 208.
25 Battestin uses "resurrect" ("Sterne among the Philosophes," 18).
26 Sterne, *Letters*, 642.
27 Sterne, *Sentimental Journey*, 2.134.
28 Sterne, *Sentimental Journey*, 2.134.
29 Sterne, *Sentimental Journey*, 2.138.
30 Sterne, *Sentimental Journey*, 2.139.
31 Sterne, *Tristram Shandy*, 5.17
32 Wilbur Cross, *Life and Times of Laurence Sterne* (New York: Macmillan, 1909), 435.
33 Sterne, *Sentimental Journey*, 2.129.
34 Sterne, *Sentimental Journey*, 1.5, 1.26–7, 2.151.
35 Shakespeare, *Hamlet*, 1.4.40.
36 Burton, *The Anatomy of Melancholy*, 249–50. See also Janine Riviere, *Dreams in Early Modern England* (London: Routledge, 2017), 149–51. On theosophy, see Jane Lead, *Fountain of Gardens* (London: J. Bradford, 1696), 372.
37 Sterne, *Sentimental Journey*, 2.122.
38 See W.G. Day, "*Tactus Interruptus* as Sternean Trope," in *Laurence Sterne and Humour*, 93–106.
39 Sterne, *Sentimental Journey*, 2.151.
40 See John Dussinger, "The Sensorium in the World of *A Sentimental Journey*," *Ariel* 13 (1982): 3–16.

41 See Thomas Cathcart and Daniel Klein, *Using Philosophy (and Jokes!) to Explore Life, Death, the Afterlife, and Everything in Between* (New York: Penguin, 2010), 103. See also Cathcart and Klein, *Understanding Philosophy through Jokes* (New York: Penguin, 2008).
42 Swift, *A Tale of a Tub and Other Works*, ed. Marcus Walsh (Cambridge: Cambridge University Press, 2010), 110.
43 Sterne, *Sentimental Journey*, 2.112.
44 Sterne, *Sentimental Journey*, 2.151.
45 Lewis, *The Great Divorce* (New York: HarperCollins, 2001), 80.
46 Lewis, *The Great Divorce*, 68.
47 Sterne, *Sentimental Journey*, 2.146–47.
48 Sterne, *Letters*, 645–6.
49 1 Samuel 28: 3–25.
50 Sterne might also be alluding to Matthew 14:26 and Mark 6:49, where the disciples temporarily mistake Jesus for a "ghost."
51 Sterne, *Sentimental Journey*, 1.45.
52 Fielding, *Tom Thumb and the Tragedy of Tragedies*, ed. L.J. Morrissey (Berkeley: University of California Press, 1970), 2.4.11.
53 Fielding, *The Tragedy of Tragedies*, 3.2.10. In addition to Shakespeare's *Macbeth*, Fielding parodies Dryden's *Conquest of Granada* (1672), where the ghost of Almanzor's mother appears, and where Almanzor vows to return as a ghost and pursue the object of his affection—Almahide— in the bedroom (Act 4, Scene 2). On Dryden and ghosts, see Jack Armistead, *Otherworldly John Dryden* (London: Routledge, 2014), 72–3.
54 Fielding, *The Tragedy of Tragedies*, 83.
55 Fielding, *The History of Tom Jones, a Foundling*, ed. Thomas Keymer and Alice Wakely (New York: Penguin, 2005), 353–4.
56 Woolf, *The Common Reader, Second Series*, ed. Andrew McNeillie (New York: Harcourt, Brace, and Jovanovich, 1984), 79.
57 Shakespeare, *Macbeth*, 1.3.79.
58 Daniel Defoe, *A View of the Invisible World* (London: s.n., 1752), 103.
59 Joseph Glanvill, *Some Philosophical Considerations Touching the Being of Witches and Witchcraft* (London: James Collins, 1667), 4.

60 Nietzsche, *Human All Too Human*, 238–9.
61 C.S. Lewis, *Surprised by Joy: The Shape of My Early Life* (London: Houghton Mifflin Harcourt, 1955), 185.

Chapter 6

1 Sterne, *Sentimental Journey*, 2.111.
2 Sterne, *Tristram Shandy*, 1.4.5.
3 Macksey, "'Alas, Poor Yorick': Sterne Thoughts," *Modern Language Notes* 98.5 (1983): 1006–20.
4 Sterne, *Sentimental Journey*, 1.84.
5 Shakespeare, *Hamlet*, 1.3.78.
6 Shakespeare, *Hamlet*, 1.3.78.
7 Sterne, *Sermons*, 5.50.
8 Sterne, *Sermons*, 4.31.
9 Hawthorne, *The Scarlet Letter* (Cambridge, MA: Harvard University Press, 2009), 216.
10 Sterne, *Sermons*, 20.189. See also Robert Walker, "Sterne's Mummies: Fraudulent Trade in 'The Prodigal Son' Sermon," *The Scriblerian and the Kit-Cats* 50.2 (2018): 156–60.
11 Chesterton, *Orthodoxy*, 8.
12 Sterne, *Sentimental Journey*, 2.155.
13 Shakespeare, *Hamlet*, 3.4.141–3.
14 Sterne, *Tristram Shandy*, 9.1.736.
15 On the king's ghost, see C.S. Lewis, "Hamlet: The Prince or the Poem?" in *Selected Literary Essays*, ed. Walter Hooper (Cambridge: Cambridge University Press, 1969), 88–105.
16 Ambrose Bierce, *The Unabridged Devil's Dictionary*, 200.
17 Sterne, *Tristram Shandy*, 1.20.64.
18 Juvenal, *The Satires*, trans. Niall Rudd (Oxford: Oxford University Press, 2008), 4.
19 Sterne, *Sentimental Journey*, 1.37.
20 Lewis, *Screwtape Letters*, 87.

21 Sterne, *Sentimental Journey*, 1.37.
22 Sterne, *Sentimental Journey*, 1.38.
23 Sterne, *Sentimental Journey*, 1.37–8.
24 Sterne, *Bramine's Journal*, 169.
25 Sterne, *Sermons*, 2.12–20.
26 Quoted in Goodwin, *The Political Genius of Abraham Lincoln*, 488.
27 Matthew 22:39; John 13:35.
28 Sterne, *Sentimental Journey*, 1.54.
29 See Kraft, *Sterne Revisited*, 112.
30 Sterne, *Sentimental Journey*, 2.111.
31 Sterne, *Sentimental Journey*, 2.111.
32 Sterne, *Sentimental Journey*, 1.77, 1.44. On Sterne's attention to gestures, see Paul Goring, *The Rhetoric of Sensibility in Eighteenth-Century Culture* (Cambridge: Cambridge University Press, 2005), 183–4.
33 Lucian, *The Way to Write History*, trans. H.W. and F.G. Fowler (Oxford: The Clarendon Press, 1905), 128.
34 Quoted in Jack Lynch, "Sterne among the Renaissance Encyclopedists," *Eighteenth-Century Fiction* 13.1 (2000): 5.
35 Ian Jack, "Introduction," in *A Sentimental Journey*, ed. Ian Jack (Oxford: Oxford University Press, 1984), xviii.
36 Sterne, *Sentimental Journey*, 2.116.
37 Thomas Gray, "Elegy Written in a Country Churchyard," in *The Oxford Book of English Verse, 1250–1900*, ed. Arthur Thomas Quiller-Couch (Oxford: The Clarendon Press, 1901), 517.
38 Sterne, *Sentimental Journey*, 1.36.
39 Cervantes, *Don Quixote*, trans. Peter Motteux, rev. John Ozell (London: D. Midwinter, 1743), II.III.40.
40 Sterne, *Sentimental Journey*, 1.27.
41 Sterne, *Bramine's Journal*, 197.
42 Sterne, *Bramine's Journal*, 197.
43 Homer, *Iliad*, trans. George Chapman (Hertfordshire: Wordsworth, 2003), 22.135.
44 Virginia Woolf, *The Common Reader, Second Series*, 72.
45 Sterne, *Tristram Shandy*, 7.43.649–51.

46 Sterne, *Sentimental Journey*, 2.159.
47 Sterne, *Sentimental Journey*, 2.159.
48 Sterne, *Sentimental Journey*, 2.159.
49 Swift, *Gulliver's Travels*, ed. Philip Smith (New York: Dover, 1996), 25–6.
50 Sterne, *Sermons*, 25.241.
51 Sterne, *Sentimental Journey*, 1.9.
52 Sterne, *Sentimental Journey*, 1.10.
53 Sterne, *Sentimental Journey*, 1.10.
54 Sterne, *Sentimental Journey*, 1.11.
55 Sterne, *Sermons*, 14.133.
56 Sterne, *Sentimental Journey*, 1.8.
57 Sterne, *Sentimental Journey*, 1.27.
58 1 Corinthians 13:1.
59 Gardiner Stout, "Yorick's *Sentimental Journey*: A Comic 'Pilgrim's Progress' for the Man of Feeling," *English Literary History* 30.4 (1963): 395–412.
60 Sterne, *Sentimental Journey*, 1.36.
61 1 Peter 4:6: "For this cause was the gospel preached also to those who are dead."
62 Kraft, "The Pentecostal Moment in *A Sentimental Journey*," in *Critical Essays on Laurence Sterne*, ed. Melvyn New (New York: Twayne, 1998), 292–310.
63 Sterne, *Sentimental Journey*, 1.58.
64 Sterne, *Tristram Shandy*, 6.17.524.
65 Sterne, *Sentimental Journey*, 1.58.
66 Sterne, *Tristram Shandy*, 9.8.754.

Chapter 7

1 Stevenson, "Sterne: Comedian and Experimental Novelist," in *The Columbia History of the British Novel*, ed. John Richetti, John Bender, Deirdre David, and Michael Seidel (New York: Columbia University Press, 1994), 154.

2   Oscar Wilde, "*Epistola: in carcere et vinculus*," in *The Complete Works of Oscar Wilde*, Volume 2, ed. Ian Small (Oxford: Oxford University Press, 2005), 39.
3   Alain de Botton, *Atheism 2.0* TED Global, 2011. On devotional reading, see Paul Griffiths, *Religious Reading* (Oxford: Oxford University Press, 1999).
4   On some of Sterne's early imitators see Mary Newbould, *Adaptations of Laurence Sterne's Fiction: Sterneana, 1760–1840* (London: Routledge, 2013). See also *Shandean Humour in English and German Literature and Philosophy*, ed. Klaus Vieweg, James Vigus, and Kathleen Wheeler (London: Routledge, 2013).
5   Thomas More, "St. Thomas More's Prayer for Good Humor," quoted in *Aleteia*, December 23, 2014: Aleteia.org.
6   J.T. Parnell, "A Story Painted to the Heart? *Tristram Shandy* and Sentimentalism Reconsidered," *Shandean* 9 (1997): 126.
7   I am indebted, here, to the religious turn in contemporary literary theory, or what others describe as "the postsecular conversation." See, for example, Bloomsbury's *New Directions in Religion and Literature* series, beginning with *Rethinking Religion and Literature*, ed. Emma Mason (London: Bloomsbury, 2015). See also *The Routledge Companion to Literature and Religion*, ed. Mark Knight (New York: Routledge, 2016); *The Cambridge Companion to Literature and Religion*, ed. Susan Felch, especially the essays by Felch, Rowan Williams, and James Matthew Wilson (Cambridge: Cambridge University Press, 2016); *The Oxford Handbook of English Literature and Theology*, ed. Andrew Haas, David Jasper, and Elisabeth Jay (Oxford: Oxford University Press, 2009); Mark Knight, *An Introduction to Religion and Literature* (London: Continuum, 2009); George Marsden, *The Outrageous Idea of Christian Scholarship* (Oxford: Oxford University Press, 1998).
8   Melvyn New, "The Odd Couple: Laurence Sterne and John Norris of Bemerton," *Philological Quarterly* 75.3 (1996): 374.
9   Richard Lanham, *Tristram Shandy: The Games of Pleasure* (Berkeley: University of California Press, 1973), 116.

10 Lewis, *Surprised by Joy*, 115.
11 Lewis, *Surprised by Joy*, 115–16.
12 Lewis, *Surprised by Joy*, 116.
13 Lewis, *Surprised by Joy*, 117.
14 F.R. Leavis, *The Great Tradition* (London: Faber & Faber, 1948), 2.
15 Quoted in James Pearson, "The Legacy of C.S. Lewis," *Modern Age* 33.4 (1991): 409.
16 Sterne, *Tristram Shandy*, 1.11.28–9.
17 Sterne, *Tristram Shandy*, 7.43.650.

Bibliography

Allen, Dennis. "Textuality/Sexuality in *Tristram Shandy*." *Studies in English Literature, 1500–1900* 25.3 (1985): 651–70.

Almond, Philip. *God: A New Biography*. London: I.B. Tauris, 2018.

Anderson, Emily Hodgson. "Theatrical Tristram: Sterne and *Hamlet* Reconsidered." *Eighteenth-Century Fiction* 27.3–4 (2015): 661–80.

Anderson, Misty. *Imagining Methodism in Eighteenth-Century Britain*. Baltimore, MD: Johns Hopkins University Press, 2012.

Anselment, Raymond. *Marprelate, Milton, Marvell, Swift and the Decorum of Religious Ridicule*. Toronto: University of Toronto Press, 1979.

Armistead, Jack. *Otherworldly John Dryden: Occult Rhetoric in His Poems and Plays*. London: Routledge, 2014.

Asfour, Lana. *Laurence Sterne in France*. New York: Continuum, 2008.

Auden, W.H. *Collected Poems*. Edited Edward Mendelson. New York: Penguin, 2007.

Bandry-Scubbi, Anne and Peter de Voogd, editors. *Hilarion's Asse: Laurence Sterne and Humour*. Newcastle: Cambridge Scholars Press, 2013.

Bath, Jo and John Newton. "Ghost Belief during the Later Seventeenth Century." *Folklore* 117.1 (2006): 1–14.

Battestin, Martin. "The Critique of Freethinking from Swift to Sterne." *Eighteenth-Century Fiction* 15.3–4 (2003): 339–420.

Battestin, Martin. "Sterne among the Philosophes: Body and Soul in *A Sentimental Journey*." *Eighteenth-Century Fiction* 7.1 (1994): 17–36.

Battestin, Martin. "*A Sentimental Journey*: Sterne's 'Work of Redemption.'" *Revue de la Société d'études anglo-américaines des XVIIe et XVIIIe siècles* 38 (1994): 189–204.

Bell, Michael. "Laurence Sterne and the Fiction of Sentiment." In *The Cambridge Companion to European Novelists*. Edited by Michael Bell. Cambridge: Cambridge University Press, 2012, 107–23.

Bellman, Patrizia Nerozzi. "The Sermons: Religious Discourse versus Modern Fiction." *The Shandean* 26 (2015): 49–54.

Berra, Yogi. *The Yogi Book*. New York: Workman Publishing Company, 2010.

Bierce, Ambrose. *The Unabridged Devil's Dictionary* (1911). Edited by David Schultz and S.J. Joshi. Athens: University of Georgia Press, 2000.

Black, Andrew. "Anti-Methodists and the Rhetoric of Methodist Spirituality." *Eighteenth-Century Life* 43.1 (2019): 76–98.

Bloom, Edward and Lillian Bloom. "Hostage to Fortune: Time, Chance, and Laurence Sterne." *Modern Philology* 85.4 (1988): 499–513.

Bobker, Danielle. "Carriages, Conversation, and *A Sentimental Journey*." *Studies in Eighteenth-Century Culture* 35.2 (2006): 243–66.

Bonds, Mark Evan. "Haydn, Laurence Sterne, and the Origins of Musical Irony." *Journal of the American Musicological Society* 44.1 (1991): 57–91.

Booth, Wayne. "Did Sterne Complete *Tristram Shandy*?" *Modern Philology* 48.3 (1951): 172–83.

Bosch, René. *Labyrinth of Digressions:* Tristram Shandy *as Perceived and Influenced by Sterne's Early Imitators*. Amsterdam: Rodopi, 2007.

Boswell, James. *Life of Johnson*. Edited by R.W. Chapman and Rev. J.D. Fleeman. Oxford: Oxford University Press, 1970.

Bowden, Martha F. *Yorick's Congregation: The Church of England in the Time of Laurence Sterne*. Newark, NJ: University of Delaware Press, 2007.

Boyle, Frank. *Swift As Nemesis: Modernity and Its Satirist*. Palo Alto, CA: Stanford University Press, 2000.

Brady, Frank. "*Tristram Shandy*: Sexuality, Morality, and Sensibility." *Eighteenth-Century Studies* 4 (1970): 41–56.

Branch, Lori. "Postsecular Studies." In *The Routledge Companion to Literature and Religion*. Edited by Mark Knight. New York: Routledge, 2016, 91–101.

Branch, Lori and Mark Knight. "Why the Postsecular Matters: Literary Studies and the Rise of the Novel." *Christianity and Literature* 67.3 (2018): 493–510.

Brown, Homer Obed. "Tristram to the Hebrews: Some Notes on the Institution of a Canonic Text." *Modern Language Notes* 99.4 (1984): 727–47.

Browne, Thomas. *Religio Medici*. London: Printed for Andrew Crooke, 1642.

Bulman, William and Robert G. Ingram, editors. *God in the Enlightenment*. Oxford: Oxford University Press, 2016.

Burchardt, Sigurd. "*Tristram Shandy*'s Law of Gravity." *English Literary History* 28.1 (1961): 70–88.

Burton, Robert. *The Anatomy of Melancholy*. Edited by Holbrook Jackson. New York: New York Review of Books Classics, 2001.

Busch, Werner. *Great Wits Jump: Laurence Sterne und die bildende Kunst*. Munich: Verlag, 2011.

Byrd, Max. *Tristram Shandy*. London: Unwin Hyman, 1985.

Carey, Brycchan. *British Abolitionism and the Rhetoric of Sensibility*. New York: Palgrave, 2005.

Carey, Daniel, "Travellers and Travel Narratives in the Early Royal Society." *Annals of Science* 54.3 (1997): 269–92.

Carmichael, Calum. "A Ceremonial Crux: Removing a Man's Sandal as a Female Gesture of Contempt." *Journal of Biblical Literature* 96.3 (1977): 321–36.

Cash, Arthur. "Sterne, Hall, Libertinism, and *A Sentimental Journey*." *The Age of Johnson* 12 (2001): 291–327.

Cash, Arthur. *Laurence Sterne: The Later Years*. London: Methuen, 1986.

Cash, Arthur. *Sterne's Comedy of Moral Sentiments: The Ethical Dimension of the Journey*. Pittsburgh: Duquesne University Press, 1966.

Cash, Arthur. "The Sermon in *Tristram Shandy*." *English Literary History* 31.4 (1964): 395–417.

Cash, Arthur. "The Lockean Psychology of *Tristram Shandy*." *English Literary History* 22.2 (1955): 125–35.

Cash, Arthur and John Stedmond, editors. *The Winged Skull: Bicentenary Conference Papers on Laurence Sterne*. London: Methuen, 1971.

Cathcart, Thomas and Daniel Klein. *Heidegger and a Hippo Walk through Those Pearly Gates: Using Philosophy (and Jokes!) to Explore Life, Death, the Afterlife, and Everything in Between*. New York: Penguin, 2010.

Cathcart, Thomas and Daniel Klein. *Plato and a Platypus Walk into a Bar: Understanding Philosophy through Jokes*. New York: Penguin, 2008.

Cervantes, Miguel de. *Don Quixote*. Translated by Peter Motteux and Rev. John Ozell. London: D. Midwinter, 1743.

Chadwick, Joseph. "Infinite Jest: Interpretation in Sterne's *A Sentimental Journey*." *Eighteenth-Century Studies* 12.2 (1979): 190–205.

Chambers, Ephram. *Cyclopaedia, or, An Universal Dictionary of Arts and Science*. 2 vols. London: James and John Knapton, 1728.

Chard, Chloe. "Grand and Ghostly Tours: The Topography of Memory." *Eighteenth-Century Studies* 31.1 (1997): 101–8.

Chesterton, G.K. *Orthodoxy*. New York: Dover, 2004.

Chibka, Robert. "*Tristram Shandy, Hamlet*, and the Vehicles of Memory." *Eighteenth-Century Fiction* 3.2 (1991): 125–52.

Coleridge, Henry Nelson, editor. *The Literary Remains of Samuel Taylor Coleridge*. London: Pickering, 1836.

Conrad, Peter. *Shandyism: The Character of Romantic Irony*. Oxford: Blackwell, 1978.

Conway, Alison and Corrinne Harol. "Toward a Post-Secular Eighteenth Century." *Literature Compass* 12.11 (2015): 565–74.

Conway, Alison and David Alvarez, editors. *Imagining Religious Toleration: A Literary History of an Idea, 1600–1830*. Toronto: University of Toronto Press, 2019.

Cross, Wilbur. *The Life and Times of Laurence Sterne*, 3rd ed. New Haven, CT: Yale University Press, 1929.

Dal Santo, Regina Maria. "Sterne, Tillotson, and Human Happiness." *The Shandean* 25 (2014): 41–65.

Darby, Robert. "The Circumcision Episode in *Tristram Shandy*." *Eighteenth-Century Life* 27.1 (2003): 72–84.

Dauber, Kenneth. *The Logic of Sentiment*. London: Bloomsbury, 2019.

Davidson, Arnold and Cathy Davidson. "Yorick Contra Hobbes." *The Centennial Review* 21.3 (1977): 282–93.

Davies, Paul. "Uneasiness: The Line between Sterne's Novel and Locke's Essay." *Textual Practice* 31.2 (2017): 247–64.

Day, W.G. "*Tactus Interruptus* as Sternean Trope." In *Hilarion's Asse: Laurence Sterne and Humour*. Edited by Anne Bandry-Scubbi and Peter de Voogd. Newcastle: Cambridge Scholar's Press, 2013, 93–106.

Day, W.G. "*Tristram Shandy*: Locke May Not Be the Key." In *Laurence Sterne: Riddles and Mysteries*. Edited by Valerie Myer. New York: Barnes and Noble, 1984, 75–83.

de Botton, Alain. *Atheism 2.0*. TED Global, 2011.

Defoe, Daniel. *A View of the Invisible World*. London: s.n., 1752.

DePorte, Michael. "Digressions and Madness in *A Tale of a Tub* and *Tristram Shandy*." *Huntington Library Quarterly* 34.1 (1970): 43–57.

Descargues, Madeleine. "Ignatius Sancho's Letters." *The Shandean* 3 (1991): 145-66.

de Voogd, Peter. "Sterne and Visual Culture." In *Cambridge Companion to Laurence Sterne*. Edited by Thomas Keymer. Cambridge: Cambridge University Press, 2009, 142-59.

de Voogd, Peter. "*Tristram Shandy* as Aesthetic Object." In *Laurence Sterne's Tristram Shandy: A Casebook*. Edited by Thomas Keymer. New York: Oxford University Press, 2006, 108-22.

de Voogd, Peter. "Laurence Sterne, the Marbled Page, and 'the Use of Accidents.'" *Word and Image* 1.3 (1985): 279-87.

de Voogd, Peter and John Neubauer, editors. *The Reception of Sterne in Europe*. New York: Continuum, 2004.

Dickson, Polly. "Tracing Squiggles: Laurence Sterne, E.T.A. Hoffmann, and Honoré de Balzac." *Comparative Literature* 72.1 (2020): 53-67.

Domingo, Darryl. *The Rhetoric of Diversion in English Literature and Culture, 1690-1760*. Cambridge: Cambridge University Press, 2016.

Downey, James. *The Eighteenth Century Pulpit: A Study of the Sermons of Butler, Berkeley, Secker, Sterne, Whitefield and Wesley*. Oxford: Clarendon Press, 1969.

Dreisbach, Christopher. *Your God Is Too Somber*. Eugene, OR: Wipf & Stock, 2019.

Dromart, Anne. "Motion and Humour in *Tristram Shandy*." In *Hilarion's Asse: Laurence Sterne and Humour*. Edited by Anne Bandry-Scubbi and Peter de Voogd. Newcastle: Cambridge Scholars Press, 2013, 15-24.

Dryden, John. *The Conquest of Granada*. London: T.N. for Henry Herringman, 1672.

During, Simon. "Taking Liberties: Sterne, Wilkes, and Warburton." In *Libertine Enlightenment: Sex, Liberty, and Licence in the Eighteenth Century*. Edited by Peter Cryle and Lisa O'Connell. Basingstoke: Palgrave, 2004, 15-33.

Dussinger, John. "Madness and Lust in the Age of Sensibility." In *Sensibility in Transformation*. Edited by Syndy McMillen Conger. Rutherford, NJ: Fairleigh Dickinson University Press, 1990, 85-102.

Dussinger, John. "The Sensorium in the World of *A Sentimental Journey*." *Ariel* 13 (1982): 3-16.

Eccles, Anastasia. "Formalism and Sentimentalism: Viktor Shklovsky and Laurence Sterne." *New Literary History* 47.4 (2016): 525–45.

Eliot, T.S. *Selected Prose of T.S. Eliot*. Edited by F. Kermode. London: Faber & Faber, 1975.

Ellis, Markman. *The Politics of Sensibility*. Cambridge: Cambridge University Press, 1996.

Englert, Hilary. "Object-Narrators and the Figure of Sterne." *Studies in Eighteenth-Century Culture* 37 (2008): 259–78.

Erickson, Robert. "Fictions of the Heart: Sterne, Law, and the Long Eighteenth Century." *Eighteenth-Century Fiction* 15.3–4 (2003): 559–82.

Eslinger, Lyle. "The Case of an Immodest Lady Wrestler in Deuteronomy 25: 11–12." *Vetus Testamentum* 31.3 (1981): 269–81.

Fairer, David. "Laurence Sterne, Tristram Shandy." In *A Companion to Literature from Milton to Blake*. Edited by David Womersley. London: Blackwell, 2017, 371–9.

Fanning, Christopher. "Small Particles of Eloquence: Sterne and the Scriblerian Text." *Modern Philology* 100.3 (2003): 360–92.

Fanning, Christopher. "The Things Themselves: Origins and Originality in Sterne's Sermons." *The Eighteenth Century* 40.1 (1999): 29–45.

Fanning, Christopher. "Sermons on Sermonizing: The Pulpit Rhetoric of Swift and Sterne." *Philological Quarterly* 76.4 (1997): 413–36.

Felch, Susan, editor. *The Cambridge Companion to Literature and Religion*. Cambridge: Cambridge University Press, 2016.

Ferguson, Robert. *Reason and Religion*. London: Dorman Newman, 1675.

Fielding, Henry. *The History of Tom Jones, a Foundling*. Edited by Thomas Keymer and Alice Wakely. New York: Penguin, 2005.

Fielding, Henry. *Tom Thumb and The Tragedy of Tragedies*. Edited by L.J. Morrissey. Berkeley: University of California Press, 1970.

Fielding, Henry. *Joseph Andrews* and *Shamela*. Edited by Douglas Brooks. Oxford: Oxford University Press, 1970.

Fields, James. *Yesterdays with Authors*. Boston, MA: J.R. Osgood, 1872.

Fitzgerald, Percy. *The Life of Laurence Sterne* (1864). London: Downey and Company, 1896.

Fitzpatrick, Vincent. *H.L. Mencken*. Macon, GA: Mercer University Press, 2004.

Fluchère, Henri. *Laurence Sterne: From Tristram to Yorick*. Oxford: Oxford University Press, 1965.

Folkenflik, Robert. "*Tristram Shandy* and Eighteenth-Century Narrative." In *The Cambridge Companion to Laurence Sterne*. Edited by Thomas Keymer. Cambridge: Cambridge University Press, 2009, 49–63.

Forster, E.M. *Aspects of the Novel*. New York: Harcourt, Brace & Company, 1927.

Franssen, Paul. "The Earl of Clonmell Reads Sterne." *The Shandean* 2 (1990): 152–201.

Franta, Andrew. *Systems Failure: The Uses of Disorder in English Literature*. Baltimore, MD: Johns Hopkins University Press, 2019.

Freedman, William. *Laurence Sterne and the Origins of the Musical Novel*. Athens: University of Georgia Press, 1978.

Freiburg, Rudolf. "Swift's Satire on Enthusiasm in *A Discourse concerning the Mechanical Operation of the Spirit* (1704)." In *Essays on Swift and His Contemporaries*. Edited by Kirsten Juhas, Patrick Müller, and Mascha Hansen. Frankfurt: Peter Lang, 2013, 167–89.

Friant-Kessler, Brigitte. "*Tristram Shandy*'s Mirroring Images." *Bulletin de la Société d'Etudes Anglo-Américaines des XVIIe et XVIIIe Siècles* 63 (2006): 63–84.

Fröhlich, Ida and Erkki Koskenniemi, editors. *Evil and the Devil*. London: Bloomsbury, 2019.

Frye, Northrop. "Towards Defining an Age of Sensibility." *English Literary History* 23.2 (1956): 144–52.

Gerard, W.B. "Laurence Sterne, the Apostrophe, and American Abolitionism, 1788–1831." In *Swiftly Sterneward*. Edited by Gerard, Derek Taylor, and Robert Walker. Newark, NJ: University of Delaware Press, 2011, 181–206.

Gerard, W.B. "Introduction." In *Divine Rhetoric: Essays on the Sermons of Laurence Sterne*. Edited by W.B. Gerard. Newark, NJ: University of Delaware Press, 2010, 13–42.

Gerard, W.B. "Changing Views toward Sentimentality Reflected in Visualizations of Sterne's Maria, 1773–1888." *Studies in Eighteenth-Century Culture* 34 (2005): 197–269.

Gibson, William and Joanne Begiato. *Sex and the Church in the Long Eighteenth Century*. London: Bloomsbury, 2017.

Gilad, Elon. "How the Prophet Isaiah Gave Hebrew Its Word for Vagina." *Haaretz* (September 1, 2015): Haaretz.com.

Glanvill, Joseph. *Some Philosophical Considerations Touching the Being of Witches and Witchcraft*. London: James Collins, 1667.

Göbel, Walter. "*Tristram Shandy* as a Playful Inquiry into Human Nature." *Arbeiten Aus Anglistik und Amerikanistik* 13.2 (1988): 155–81.

Goodhue, Elizabeth. "When Yorick Takes His Tea." *Journal of Early Modern Cultural Studies* 6.1 (2006): 51–83.

Goodwin, Doris Kearns. *Team of Rivals: The Political Genius of Abraham Lincoln*. New York: Simon and Schuster, 2005.

Gordon, Catherine. *British Paintings of Subjects from the English Novel, 1740–1870*. New York: Garland, 1988.

Goring, Paul. *The Rhetoric of Sensibility in Eighteenth-Century Culture*. Cambridge: Cambridge University Press, 2005.

Gow, James S. "Were Sterne's Sermons Novel?" *The Shandean* 24 (2013): 70–83.

Gow, James S. "A Brief Account of Sterne's Homiletic Piracy." In *Divine Rhetoric: Essays on the Sermons of Laurence Sterne*. Edited by W. B. Gerard. Newark, NJ: University of Delaware Press, 2010, 123–48.

Gray, Thomas. "Elegy Written in a Country Churchyard." In *The Oxford Book of English Verse, 1250–1900*. Edited by Arthur Thomas Quiller-Couch. Oxford: The Clarendon Press, 1901, 516–20.

Greene, Donald. "Latitudinarianism and Sensibility: The Genealogy of the 'Man of Feeling' Reconsidered." *Modern Philology* 75.2 (1977): 159–83.

Gregori, Flavio. "Body, Mind, Sartorial Metaphors, and Sexual Imagery in Sterne's *Tristram Shandy*." *ACME* 70.2 (2017): 29–37.

Gregori, Flavio. "Homunculus ab ovo: Beginning as Continuity and Discontinuity in *Tristram Shandy*." *Dans Études Anglaises* 66.2 (2013): 214–33.

Gregori, Flavio. "Were Sterne's Sermons Novel?" *The Shandean* 24 (2013): 70–83.

Griffiths, Paul. *Religious Reading: The Place of Reading in the Practice of Religion*. Oxford: Oxford University Press, 1999.

Haas, Andrew, David Jasper, and Elisabeth Jay, editors. *The Oxford Handbook of English Literature and Theology*. Oxford: Oxford University Press, 2007.

Hadfield, Andrew. "Sterne amongst the Philosophers." *Textual Practice* 31.2 (2017): 225–32.

Hall, Joseph. *A Just Censure of Travel, as It Is Commonly Undertaken by the Gentlemen of Our Nation*. London: Printed by Edward Griffin for Nathaniel Butter, 1617.

Hamilton, Harlan. "Sterne's Sermon in Paris and Its Background." *Proceedings of the American Philosophical Society* 128.4 (1984): 316–25.

Handley, Sasha. *Visions of an Unseen World: Ghost Beliefs and Ghost Stories in Eighteenth-Century England*. London: Pickering & Chatto, 2007.

Harkness, Deborah. *John Dee's Conversations with Angels: Cabala, Alchemy, and the End of Nature*. Cambridge: Cambridge University Press, 1999.

Harries, Elizabeth. "Words, Sex, and Gender in Sterne's Novels." In *The Cambridge Companion to Laurence Sterne*. Edited by Thomas Keymer. Cambridge: Cambridge University Press, 2009, 111–24.

Harries, Elizabeth. "Sterne's Novels: Gathering Up the Fragments." *English Literary History* 49.1 (1982): 35–49.

Hart, David Bentley. *Essays in Theology and Metaphysics*. Grand Rapids, MI: Eerdmans, 2017.

Hart, David Bentley. *The Experience of God: Being, Consciousness, Bliss*. New Haven, CT: Yale University Press, 2013.

Hartling, Shannon. "Inexpressible Sadness: Sterne's Sermons and the Moral Inadequacies of Politeness in *Tristram Shandy*." *Christianity and Literature* 55.4 (2006): 495–510.

Hartvig, Gabriella. "Early Interpretations of Sterne's 'Learned Wit' in German Aesthetics." *The Shandean* 18 (2007): 23–32.

Hauge, Matthew. *The Biblical Tour of Hell*. London: Bloomsbury, 2013.

Havard, John Owen. "Arbitrary Government: *Tristram Shandy* and the Crisis of Whig History." *English Literary History* 81.2 (2014): 585–613.

Hawley, Judith. "Tristram Shandy, Philosopher." *Textual Practice* 31.2 (2017): 233–46.

Hawley, Judith. "Sympathy and Sexuality in *Tristram Shandy*; or, Plain Stories." In *Digressions in European Literature*. Edited by Alexis Grohmann and Caragh Wells. London: Palgrave, 2011, 21–35.

Hawley, Judith. "*Tristram Shandy*, Learned Wit, and Enlightenment Knowledge." In *The Cambridge Companion to Laurence Sterne*. Edited by Thomas Keymer. Cambridge: Cambridge University Press, 2009, 34–48.

Hawthorne, Nathaniel. *The Scarlet Letter*. Cambridge, MA: Harvard University Press, 2009.

Haynes, Cynthia. "Grand Tourists and Anti-Catholicism after 1745." *Journal for Eighteenth-Century Studies* 33.2 (2010): 195–208.

Hobbes, Thomas. *Leviathan*, ed. C.B. MacPherson. London: Penguin, 1985.

Holden, Charlotte. "'Against the Spleen': *Tristram Shandy*, Jest-Books and Treatment for Melancholy." *Revue de la Société d'études anglo-américaines des XVIIe et XVIIIe siècles* 70 (2013): 153–75.

Holland, Norman. "The Laughter of Laurence Sterne." *The Hudson Review* 9.3 (1956): 422–30.

Holland, William, editor. *The Beauties of Sterne*. London: C. Etherington, 1782.

Holm, Melanie. "Laughter, Skepticism, and the Pleasures of Being Misunderstood in Laurence Sterne's *The Life and Opinions of Tristram Shandy, Gentleman*." *The Eighteenth Century* 55.4 (2014): 355–75.

Homer. *Iliad*, trans. George Chapman. Hertfordshire: Wordsworth, 2003.

Hopkins, David. "Classical Translation and Imitation." In *A Companion to Literature from Milton to Blake*. Edited by David Womersley. Oxford: Blackwell, 2000, 76–93.

Howes, Alan B., editor. *Laurence Sterne: The Critical Heritage*. London: Routledge, 1974.

Hume, David. *An Enquiry Concerning the Principles of Morals*. Edited by L.A. Selby-Bigge and P.H. Nidditch. Oxford: Oxford University Press, 1975.

Hume, David. *Letters of David Hume*. Edited by J.Y.T. Greig. Oxford: Oxford University Press, 1932.

Hunter, J. Paul. "Formalism and History." *Modern Language Quarterly* 61.1 (2000): 109–29.

Hunter, J. Paul. "The Troubles of Tristram and the Aesthetics of Uncertainty." In *Rhetorics of Order/Ordering Rhetorics in English Neoclassical Literature*. Edited by J. Douglas Canfield and J. Paul Hunter. Newark, NJ: University of Delaware Press, 1989, 173–98.

Hunter, J. Paul. "Response as Reformation: *Tristram Shandy* and the Art of Interruption." *Novel: A Forum on Fiction* 4.2 (1971): 132–46.

Iser, Wolfgang. *Laurence Sterne: Tristram Shandy*. Cambridge: Cambridge University Press, 1988.

Jack, Ian and Tim Parnell, editors. *A Sentimental Journey and Other Writings*. Oxford: Oxford University Press, 2003.

Jackson, H.J. "Sterne, Burton, and Ferriar: Allusions to the Anatomy of Melancholy in Volumes Five to Nine of *Tristram Shandy*." *Philological Quarterly* 54.2 (1975): 457–70.

Jacobs, Alan. *A Theology of Reading: The Hermeneutics of Love*. New York: Westview Press, 2001.

Jasper, David. "Echoes of God's Laughter: Why Theologians Should Read Novels." *Theology* 106.6 (2003): 414–20.

Jasper, David. *The Study of Literature and Religion*. London: Palgrave, 1992.

Jefferson, Douglas. "*Tristram Shandy* and the Tradition of Learned Wit." *Essays in Criticism* 1 (1951): 225–48.

Jefferson, Thomas. "Letter to Peter Carr." August 10, 1787.

John Paul II. *Theology of the Body*. Rome: Libreria Editrice Vaticana, 2005.

Jones, Darrell. "Locke and Sterne: The History of a Critical Hobby-Horse." *The Shandean* 27 (2016): 83–111.

Joseph, Sister Miriam. "Discerning the Ghost in *Hamlet*." *PMLA* 76.5 (1961): 493–502.

Joyce, James. *James Joyce: Two Decades of Criticism*. Edited by Seon Givens. New York: Vanguard Press, 1948.

Juvenal. *The Satires*. Translated by Niall Rudd. Oxford: Oxford University Press, 2008.

Kaltner, John, Steven McKenzie, and Joel Kilpatrick. *The Uncensored Bible: The Bawdy and Naughty Bits of the Good Book*. New York: HarperOne, 2008.

Keymer, Thomas. "*A Sentimental Journey* and the Failure of Feeling." In *The Cambridge Companion to Laurence Sterne*. Edited by Keymer. Cambridge: Cambridge University Press, 2009, 79–94.

Keymer, Thomas. *Joseph Andrews and Shamela*. Oxford: Oxford University Press, 2008.

Keymer, Thomas. *Sterne, the Moderns, and the Novel*. Oxford: Oxford University Press, 2002.

Keymer, Thomas. "Marvell, Thomas Hollis, and Sterne's Maria: Parody in *A Sentimental Journey*." *The Shandean* 5 (1993): 9–31.

Knight, Mark, editor. *The Routledge Companion to Literature and Religion*. New York: Routledge, 2016.

Knight, Mark. *An Introduction to Religion and Literature*. London: Continuum, 2009.

Knights, Mark and Adam Morton, editors. *The Power of Laughter and Satire in Early Modern Britain*. London: Boydell & Brewer, 2017.

Korkowski, Eugene. "The 'Second *Tale of a Tub*': A Link from Swift to Sterne?" *Studies in the Novel* 6.4 (1974): 470–4.

Korshin, Paul. *Typologies in England, 1650–1820*. Princeton, NJ: Princeton University Press, 1982.

Kraft, Elizabeth. "Bohemian Sterne." In *Sterne, Tristram, Yorick: Tercentenary Essays on Laurence Sterne*. Edited by Melvyn New, Peter de Voogd, and Judith Hawley. Newark, NJ: University of Delaware Press, 2015, 25–40.

Kraft, Elizabeth. "Laurence Sterne and the Ethics of Sexual Difference." *Christianity and Literature* 51.3 (2002): 363–85.

Kraft, Elizabeth. "The Pentecostal Moment in *A Sentimental Journey*." In *Critical Essays on Laurence Sterne*. Edited by Melvyn New. New York: Twayne, 1998, 292–310.

Kraft, Elizabeth. *Laurence Sterne Revisited*. London: Twayne, 1996.

Lamb, Jonathan. "The Job Controversy, Sterne, and the Question of Allegory." *Eighteenth-Century Studies* 24.1 (1990): 1–19.

Lamb, Jonathan. *Sterne's Fiction and the Double Principle*. Cambridge: Cambridge University Press, 1989.

Lamb, Jonathan. "Sterne's System of Imitation." *The Modern Language Review* 76.4 (1981): 794–810.

Lane, Belden. "Language, Metaphor, and Pastoral Theology." *Theology Today* 43.4 (1987): 487–502.

Lanham, Richard. *Tristram Shandy: The Games of Pleasure*. Berkeley: University of California Press, 1973.

Law, Jules David. *The Rhetoric of Empiricism: Language and Perception from Locke to I.A. Richard*. Ithaca, NY: Cornell University Press, 1993.

Lead, Jane. *Fountain of Gardens*. London: J. Bradford, 1696.

Leavis, F.R. *The Great Tradition*. London: Faber & Faber, 1948.

Lemon, Rebecca, Emma Mason, Jonathan Roberts, Christopher Rowland, editors. *The Blackwell Companion to the Bible in English Literature*. Oxford: Blackwell, 2009.

Levack, Brian. *The Devil Within: Possession and Exorcism in the Christian West*. New Haven, CT: Yale University Press, 2013.

Lewis, C.S. *The Screwtape Letters*. New York: HarperOne, 2015.

Lewis, C.S. *Of Other Worlds: Essays and Stories*. Edited by W. Hooper. New York: Harcourt, 2002.

Lewis, C.S. *The Great Divorce*. New York: HarperCollins, 2001.

Lewis, C.S. *Mere Christianity*. New York: HarperOne, 2000.

Lewis, C.S. *The Weight of Glory and Other Addresses*. New York: HarperOne, 1980.

Lewis, C.S. "Hamlet: The Prince or the Poem?" In *Selected Literary Essays*. Edited by Walter Hooper. Cambridge: Cambridge University Press, 1969, 88–105.

Lewis, C.S. *Surprised by Joy: The Shape of My Early Life*. London: Houghton Mifflin Harcourt, 1955.

Lewis, Jayne. *Air's Appearance: Literary Atmosphere in British Fiction, 1660–1794*. Chicago, IL: University of Chicago Press, 2012.

Lindvall, Terry. *Surprised by Laughter: The Comic World of C.S. Lewis*. New York: Thomas Nelson, 2012.

Lipski, Jakub. *In Quest of the Self: Masquerade and Travel in the Eighteenth-Century Novel: Fielding, Smollett, Sterne*. Amsterdam: Rodopi, 2014.

Lobis, Seth. *The Virtue of Sympathy: Magic, Philosophy, and Literature in Seventeenth-Century England*. New Haven, CT: Yale University Press, 2015.

Lounsberry, Barbara. "Sermons and Satire: Anti-Catholicism in Sterne." *Philological Quarterly* 55.3 (1976): 403–17.

Loveridge, Mark. *Laurence Sterne and the Argument about Design*. London: Macmillan, 1982.

Lovesey, Oliver. "Divine Enthusiasm and Love Melancholy: *Tristram Shandy* and Eighteenth-Century Narratives of Saint Errantry." *Eighteenth-Century Fiction* 16.3 (2004): 373–99.

Lucian. *The Way to Write History*. Translated by H.W. and F.G. Fowler. Oxford: The Clarendon Press, 1905.

Lund, Roger. *Ridicule, Religion and the Politics of Wit in Augustan England*. Farnham: Ashgate, 2012.

Lund, Roger. *The Margins of Orthodoxy: Heterodox Writing and Cultural Response, 1660–1750*. Cambridge: Cambridge University Press, 1995.

Lupton, Christina. "*Tristram Shandy*, David Hume and Epistemological Fiction." *Philosophy and Literature* 27.1 (2003): 98–115.

Lynch, Jack. "Sterne among the Renaissance Encyclopedists." *Eighteenth-Century Fiction* 13.1 (2000): 1–18.

Macksey, Richard. "'Alas, Poor Yorick': Sterne Thoughts." *Modern Language Notes* 98.5 (1983): 1006–20.

MacLean, Kenneth. "Imagination and Sympathy: Sterne and Adam Smith." *Journal of the History of Ideas* 10.3 (1949): 399–410.

Maioli, Roger. *Empiricism and the Early Theory of the Novel*. New York: Palgrave, 2016.

Marsden, George. *The Outrageous Idea of Christian Scholarship*. Oxford: Oxford University Press, 1998.

Marshall, Ashley. "Thinking about Satire." In *The Oxford Handbook of Eighteenth-Century Satire*. Edited by Paddy Bullard. Oxford: Oxford University Press, 2019, 475–91.

Martin, Michael. *Literature and the Encounter with God in Post-Reformation England*. London: Routledge, 2014.

Mason, Emma. "Rethinking Religion and Literature." In *Reading the Abrahamic Faiths: Rethinking Religion and Literature*. Edited by Emma Mason. London: Bloomsbury, 2015, 3–16.

Matalene, H.W. "Sexual Scripting in Montaigne and Sterne." *Comparative Literature* 41.4 (1989): 360–77.

Matytsin, Anton. *The Specter of Skepticism in the Age of Enlightenment*. Baltimore, MD: Johns Hopkins University Press, 2016.

Mazella, David. "The Perils of Didacticism in *Tristram Shandy*." *Studies in the Novel* 31. 2 (1999): 152–77.

McDannell, Colleen and Bernhard Lang. *Heaven: A History*. New Haven, CT: Yale University Press, 2001.

McGlynn, Paul. "Sterne's Maria: Madness and Sentimentality." *Eighteenth-Century Life* 3.2 (1976): 39–43.

McGlynn, Paul. "Orthodoxy versus Anarchy in Sterne's *Sentimental Journey*." *Papers on Language and Literature* 7.3 (1971): 242–51.

Mellier, Denis. "The Origins of Adult Graphic Narratives: Graphic Literature and the Novel, from Laurence Sterne to Gustave Doré (1760–1851)." In *The Cambridge History of the Graphic Novel*. Edited by Jan Baetens, Hugo Frey, and Stephen E. Tabachnick. Cambridge: Cambridge University Press, 2018, 21–38.

Moglen, Helene. *The Philosophical Irony of Laurence Sterne*. Gainesville: University of Florida Press, 1975.

Moland, Lydia, editor. *All Too Human: Laughter, Humor, and Comedy in Nineteenth-Century Philosophy*. Boston, MA: Springer, 2018.

Molesworth, Jesse. *Chance and the Eighteenth-Century Novel: Realism, Probability, Magic*. Cambridge: Cambridge University Press, 2010.

Monod, Paul Kléber. *Solomon's Secret Arts: The Occult in the Age of Enlightenment*. New Haven, CT: Yale University Press, 2013.

Moore, Paul. "Sterne, Tristram, Yorick, Birds, and Beasts." *Journal for Eighteenth-Century Studies* 10.1 (1987): 43–54.

More, Thomas. *The Complete Works of Thomas More*, Volume 12. Edited by Louis L. Martz and Frank Manley. New Haven, CT: Yale University Press, 1976.

Moss, Robert. "Sterne's Punctuation." *Eighteenth-Century Studies* 15.2 (1982): 179–200.

Mullan, John. "The Life and Opinions of Laurence Sterne: The First Unapologetic Literary Celebrity." *The Guardian* (March 15, 2018): theguardian.com.

Mullan, John. "Sterne's Comedy of Sentiments." *Revue de la Société d'études anglo-américaines des XVIIe et XVIIIe siècles* 38 (1994): 233–41.

Mullan, John. *Sentiment and Sociability: The Language of Feeling in the Eighteenth Century*. Oxford: Oxford University Press, 1988.

Müller, Patrick. *Latitudinarianism and Didacticism in Eighteenth Century Literature: Moral Theology in Fielding, Sterne, and Goldsmith*. Frankfurt: Peter Lang, 2009.

Nagle, Christopher. "Sterne, Shelley, and Sensibility's Pleasures of Proximity." *English Literary History* 70.3 (2003): 813–45.

New, Melvyn. "Sterne's Bawdry: A Cautionary Tale." *Review of English Studies* 62 (2010): 80–9.

New, Melvyn. "The Odd Couple: Laurence Sterne and John Norris of Bemerton." *Philological Quarterly* 75.3 (1996): 361–85.

New, Melvyn. "A Note on Annotating *Tristram Shandy*." In *Laurence Sterne: Riddles and Mysteries*. Edited by Valerie Grosvenor Myer. Totowa, NJ: Barnes and Noble, 1984, 15–23.

New, Melvyn. "Sterne, Warburton, and the Burden of Exuberant Wit." *Eighteenth-Century Studies* 15 (1982): 245–74.

New, Melvyn. "Sterne's Rabelaisian Fragment: A Text from the Holograph Manuscript." *PMLA* 87.5 (1972): 1083–92.

New, Melvyn. *Laurence Sterne as Satirist: A Reading of* Tristram Shandy. Gainesville: University of Florida Press, 1969.

Newbould, Mary and W.B. Gerard, editors. *Laurence Sterne's* A Sentimental Journey. Lewisburg: Bucknell University Press, 2021.

Newbould, Mary. "The Beauties of Fielding and Sterne." In *The Afterlives of Eighteenth-Century Fiction*. Edited by Daniel Cook and Nicholas Seager. Cambridge: Cambridge University Press, 2015, 133–52.

Newbould, Mary. *Adaptations of Laurence Sterne's Fiction: Sterneana, 1760–1840*. London: Routledge, 2013.

Newbould, Mary. "Caricature in Sterne's Fictional Worlds." In *Hilarion's Asse: Laurence Sterne and Humour*. Edited by Anne Bandry-Scubbi and Peter de Voogd. Newcastle: Cambridge Scholars Press, 2013, 37–52.

Newbould, Mary. "Shandying It Away: Sterne's Theatricality." *The Shandean* 18 (2007): 156–70.

Nietzsche, Friedrich. *Human All Too Human: A Book for Free Spirits*. Translated by R.J. Hollingdale. Cambridge: Cambridge University Press, 1996.

Norton, Brian Michael. "The Moral in Phutatorius's Breeches: *Tristram Shandy* and the Limits of Stoic Ethics." *Eighteenth Century Fiction* 18.4 (2006): 405–23.

Nowka, Scott. "Satirizing Materialism in Gildon and Sterne." *Eighteenth-Century Fiction* 22.2 (2009): 195–222.

Nuttall, Anthony David. *A Common Sky: Philosophy and the Literary Imagination*. London: Chatto & Windus, 1974.

Oakley, Warren. *Laurence Sterne, His Readers and the Art of Bodysnatching*. London: MHRA, 2010.

Ormsby-Lennon, Hugh. *Hey Presto!: Swift and the Quacks*. Newark, NJ: University of Delaware Press, 2011.

Palmeri, Frank. *Satire, History, Novel: Narrative Forms, 1665–1815*. Newark, NJ: University of Delaware Press, 2003.

Pappa, Joseph. *Carnal Reading*. Newark, NJ: University of Delaware Press, 2011.

Parker, Fred. *Scepticism and Literature: An Essay on Pope, Hume, Sterne, and Johnson*. Oxford: Oxford University Press, 2003.

Parnell, Tim. *Laurence Sterne: A Literary Life*. New York: Palgrave, 2020.

Parnell, Tim. "Sterne's Fiction and the Mid-Century Novel." In *The Oxford Handbook of the Eighteenth-Century Novel*. Edited by J.A. Downie. Oxford: Oxford University Press, 2016, 264–81.

Parnell, Tim. "The Sermons of Mr. Yorick: The Commonplace and the Rhetoric of the Heart." In *The Cambridge Companion to Laurence Sterne*. Edited by Thomas Keymer. Cambridge: Cambridge University Press, 2009, 64–78.

Parnell, Tim. "Laurence Sterne and the Problem of Belief." *Shandean* 17 (2006): 121–39.

Parnell, Tim. "*Tristram Shandy* and Sentimentalism Reconsidered." *Shandean* 9 (1997): 122–35.

Parnell, Tim. "Montaigne's *Apology*, *Hamlet* and *Tristram Shandy*: Enquiry and Sceptical Response." *Eighteenth-Century Ireland/Iris an dá chultúr* 10 (1995): 148–55.

Parnell, Tim. "Swift, Sterne, and the Skeptical Tradition." *Studies in Eighteenth-Century Culture* 23 (1994): 221–42.

Partridge, Eric. *Shakespeare's Bawdy*. New York: Routledge, 2001.

Pascal, Blaise. *Pensées*. Translated by A.J. Krailsheimer. New York: Penguin, 1995.

Patrick, Duncan. "Unorthodox Theology in Two Short Works by Sterne." *The Review of English Studies* 56 (2005): 49–58.

Patrides, C.A. *The Grand Design of God: The Literary Form of the Christian View of History*. London: Routledge, 1972.

Patrides, C.A. "The Salvation of Satan." *Journal of the History of Ideas* 28.4 (1967): 467–78.

Paulson, Ronald. *Hogarth's Harlots: Sacred Parody in Enlightenment England*. Baltimore, MD: Johns Hopkins University Press, 2003.
Pearson, James. "The Legacy of C.S. Lewis." *Modern Age* 33.4 (1991): 409–11.
Peterfreund, Stuart. "Sterne and Late Eighteenth-Century Ideas of History." *Eighteenth-Century Life* 7.1 (1981): 25–53.
Petrakis, Byron. "Jester in the Pulpit: Sterne and Pulpit Eloquence." *Philological Quarterly* 51.2 (1972): 430–47.
Petrie, Graham. "Rhetoric as Fictional Technique in *Tristram Shandy*." *Philological Quarterly* 48.4 (1969): 479–94.
Pfister, Manfred. *Laurence Sterne*. London: Northcote House, 2001.
Pierce, David and Jan de Voogd, editors. *Laurence Sterne in Modernism and Postmodernism*. Leiden: Brill, 1996.
Potkay, Adam. *The Story of Joy: From the Bible to Late Romanticism*. Cambridge: Cambridge University Press, 2007.
Prickett, Stephen. "Tradition, Preaching, and the Gothic Revival." In *The Oxford Handbook of the British Sermon 1689–1901*. Edited by Keith Francis and William Gibson. Oxford: Oxford University Press, 2012, 579–93.
Prickett, Stephen. "A Reply to Melvyn New." *Christianity and Literature* 49.1 (1999): 67–73.
Prickett, Stephen. *Origins of Narrative: The Romantic Appropriation of the Bible*. Cambridge: Cambridge University Press, 1996.
Prince, Michael. *Philosophical Dialogue in the British Enlightenment: Theology, Aesthetics, and the Novel*. Cambridge: Cambridge University Press, 1996.
Prior, Matthew. *Literary Works of Matthew Prior*. Edited by H. Bunker Wright and Monroe K. Spears. Oxford: Oxford University Press, 1959.
Purton, Valerie. *Dickens and the Sentimental Tradition*. London: Anthem Press, 2012.
Putney, Rufus. "The Evolution of *A Sentimental Journey*." *Philological Quarterly* 19 (1940): 364–7.
Rabelais, François. *Gargantua and Pantagruel* (1738). Translated by Thomas Urquhart and Peter Motteux. Edited by John Ozell. New York: Dover, 2016.
Randall, David. *The Conversational Enlightenment: The Reconception of Rhetoric in Eighteenth-Century Thought*. Edinburgh: Edinburgh University Press, 2019.

Rawson, Claude. *Satire and Sentiment, 1660–1830*. Cambridge: Cambridge University Press, 1994.

Read, Herbert. *Essays in Criticism*. Freeport, NY: Books for Libraries, 1967.

Reeves, James. *Godless Fictions in the Eighteenth Century: A Literary History of Atheism*. Cambridge: Cambridge University Press, 2020.

Regan, Shaun. "Translating Rabelais: Sterne, Motteux, and the Culture of Politeness." *Translation and Literature* 10.2 (2011): 174–99.

Richardson, John. "*Tristram Shandy* and War Representation." *Eighteenth-Century Life* 44.1 (2020): 27–48.

Richetti, John. *A History of Eighteenth-Century British Literature*. London: Wiley, 2017.

Riviere, Janine. *Dreams in Early Modern England*. London: Routledge, 2017.

Roberts, Hannah. "Spike Milligan's Gravestone Quip Is Nation's Favourite Epitaph." *Daily Mail* (May 17, 2012): dailymail.co.uk.

Roccia, Gioiella Bruni. "An Intertextual Approach to *Tristram Shandy*." *European Journal of Literature, Language and Linguistic Studies* 2.2 (2018): 35–43.

Rogers, Pat. "*Tristram Shandy's* Polite Conversation." *Essays in Criticism* 32.3 (1982): 303–20.

Rosenberg, Rabbi A.J. and Rabbi Reuven Hochberg, translators. *The Book of Kings 1: A New Translation of the Text, Rashi and a Commentary Digest*. New York: Judaica Press, 1988.

Rosenblum, Michael. "The Sermon, the King of Bohemia, and the Art of Interpolation in *Tristram Shandy*." *Studies in Philology* 75.4 (1978): 472–91.

Ross, Ian Campbell. "'Alas, poor Yorick!': Death and the Comic Novel." *Oxford University Press Blog* (March 18, 2018): blog.oup.com

Ross, Ian Campbell. *Laurence Sterne: A Life*. Oxford: Oxford University Press, 2001.

Rousseau, George. "Brain, Mind and Soul in the Long Eighteenth Century." *Journal for Eighteenth-Century Studies* 30.2 (2007): 161–91.

Russell, Jeffrey Burton. *The Devil: Perceptions of Evil from Antiquity to Primitive Christianity*. Ithaca, NY: Cornell University Press, 1987.

Seidel, Michael. *Satiric Inheritance: Rabelais to Sterne*. Princeton, NJ: Princeton University Press, 1979.

Shakespeare, William. *The Comedy of Errors*. Edited by Sylvan Barnet and Harry Levin. New York: Signet, 2002.

Shakespeare, William. *Much Ado about Nothing*. Edited by Sylvan Barnet. New York: Signet, 1998.

Shakespeare, William. *Macbeth*. Edited by Sylvan Barnet. New York: Signet, 1998.

Shakespeare, William. *Hamlet*. Edited by Sylvan Barnet. New York: Signet Classic, 1998.

Shankman, Steven. "The End of Laurence Sterne's *A Sentimental Journey* and the Resistance to Doctrine." *Religion & Literature* 29.3 (1997): 43–61.

Shaw, Jane. *Miracles in Enlightenment England*. New Haven, CT: Yale University Press, 2006.

Sheehan, Jonathan. *The Enlightenment Bible*. Princeton, NJ: Princeton University Press, 2005.

Shklovsky, Viktor. "Sterne's *Tristram Shandy*: A Stylistic Commentary." In *Russian Formalist Criticism: Four Essays*. Edited by Lee Lemon and Marion Reis. Lincoln: University of Nebraska Press, 1965, 25–57.

Shuger, Debora. "The Philosophical Foundations of Sacred Rhetoric." In *Rhetorical Invention and Religious Inquiry*. Edited by Walter Jost and Wendy Olmsted. New Haven, CT: Yale University Press, 2000, 47–64.

Sichel, Walter. *Sterne: A Study*. London: Williams and Norgate, 1910.

Simms, Norman. "The Missing Jews and Jewishness in *Tristram Shandy*." *The Shandean* 4 (1992): 135–52.

Sitter, John. *Arguments of Augustan Wit*. Cambridge: Cambridge University Press, 1991.

Sluhovsky, Moche. *Believe not Every Spirit: Possession, Mysticism, and Discernment in Early Modern Catholicism*. Chicago, IL: University of Chicago Press, 2007.

Smith, Anthony Paul. "Postsecularism: Introduction." In *Reading the Abrahamic Faiths: Rethinking Religion and Literature*. Edited by Emma Mason. London: Bloomsbury, 2015, 221–37.

Snobelen, Stephen. "Isaac Newton and the Devil." In *Newton and Newtonianism: New Studies*. Edited by James E. Force and Sarah Hutton. London: Kluwer, 2004, 155–81.

South, Robert. *Forty-Eight Sermons*, 3rd ed. London: G. James, 1715.

Spacks, Patricia. *Novel Beginnings: Experiments in Eighteenth-Century English Fiction*. New Haven, CT: Yale University Press, 2006.

Spacks, Patricia. *Desire and Truth: Functions of Plot in Eighteenth-Century English Novels*. Chicago, CT: University of Chicago Press, 1990.

Stark, Ryan. "A Double Entendre in Laurence Sterne's Sermon on the Prodigal Son." *Notes and Queries* 64.3 (2017): 489–91.

Stark, Ryan. *Rhetoric, Science, and Magic in Seventeenth-Century England*. Washington, DC: Catholic University of America Press, 2009.

Staves, Susan. "*Don Quixote* in Eighteenth-Century England." *Comparative Literature* 24.3 (1972): 193–215.

Stedmond, John. *The Comic Art of Laurence Sterne: Convention and Innovation in* Tristram Shandy *and* A Sentimental Journey. Toronto: University of Toronto Press, 1967.

Stedmond, John. "Satire and *Tristram Shandy*." *Studies in English* Literature, *1500–1900*. 1.3 (1961): 53–63.

Sterne, Laurence. *The Letters of Laurence Sterne: Part One, 1739–1764*. Edited by Melvyn New and Peter de Voogd. Gainesville: University of Florida Press, 2009.

Sterne, Laurence. *The Letters of Laurence Sterne: Part Two, 1765–1768*. Edited by Melvyn New and Peter de Voogd. Gainesville: University of Florida Press, 2009.

Sterne, Laurence. *A Sentimental Journey through France and Italy and Continuation of the Bramine's Journal*. Edited by Melvyn New and W.G. Day. Gainesville: University of Florida Press, 2002.

Sterne, Laurence. *The Sermons of Laurence Sterne*. Edited by Melvyn New. Gainesville: University of Florida Press, 1996.

Sterne, Laurence. *The Sermons of Laurence Sterne: The Notes*. Edited by Melvyn New. Gainesville: University of Florida Press, 1996.

Sterne, Laurence. *The Life and Opinions of Tristram Shandy, Gentleman: The Notes*. Edited by Melvyn New, Richard A. Davies, and W.G. Day. Gainesville: University of Florida Press, 1984.

Sterne, Laurence. *The Life and Opinions of Tristram Shandy*. Edited by Melvyn New and Joan New. Gainesville: University of Florida Press, 1978.

Sterne, Laurence. *The Letters of Laurence Sterne*. Edited by Lewis P. Curtis. Oxford: Oxford University Press, 1935.

Stevenson, John Allen. "Sterne: Comedian and Experimental Novelist." In *The Columbia History of the British Novel*. Edited by John Richetti, John Bender, Deirdre David, and Michael Seidel. New York: Columbia University Press, 1994, 154–80.

Stewart, Carol. "The Anglicanism of *Tristram Shandy*: Latitudinarianism at the Limits." *Journal for Eighteenth-Century Studies* 28.2 (2005): 239–50.

Stock, Robert. *The Holy and the Daemonic from Sir Thomas Browne to William Blake*. Princeton, NJ: Princeton University Press, 1982.

Stout, Gardiner Stout, editor. *A Sentimental Journey*. Berkeley: University of California Press, 1967.

Stout, Gardiner. "Yorick's *Sentimental Journey*: A Comic *Pilgrim's Progress* for the Man of Feeling." *English Literary History* 30.4 (1963): 395–412.

Swallow, Karen Prior. "*Tristram Shandy* and the Paradox of the Incarnation." *The Shandean* 22 (2011): 116–31.

Swearingen, James. *Reflexivity in* Tristram Shandy: *An Essay in Phenomenological Criticism*. New Haven, CT: Yale University Press, 1977.

Swift, Jonathan. *A Tale of a Tub and Other Works*. Edited by Marcus Walsh. Cambridge: Cambridge University Press, 2010.

Swift, Jonathan. *A Tale of a Tub and Other Works*. Edited by Angus Ross and David Woolley. Oxford: Oxford University Press, 2008.

Swift, Jonathan. *Gulliver's Travels*, ed. Philip Smith. New York: Dover, 1996.

Tadié, Alexis. *Sterne's Whimsical Theatres of Language: Orality, Gesture, Literacy*. Aldershot: Ashgate, 2003.

Tave, Stuart. *The Amiable Humorist: A Study in the Comic Theory and Criticism of the Eighteenth and Early Nineteenth Centuries*. Chicago, IL: University of Chicago Press, 1960.

Tavor, Eve. *Scepticism, Society and the Eighteenth-Century Novel*. London: Palgrave Macmillan, 1987.

Taylor, Charles. *A Secular Age*. Cambridge, MA: Harvard University Press, 2007.

Taylor, E. Derek. "Samuel Richardson's Clarissa and the Problem of Heaven." In *Theology and Literature in the Age of Johnson*. Edited by Melvyn New and Gerard Reedy. Newark, NJ: University of Delaware Press, 2012, 71–89.

Taylor, E. Derek. *Reason and Religion in* Clarissa. London: Routledge, 2009.

Thomas, Keith. *The Ends of Life*. Oxford: Oxford University Press, 2009.

Thomas, Keith. *Religion and the Decline of Magic: Studies in Popular Beliefs in Sixteenth-and Seventeenth-Century England*. London: Weidenfeld & Nicolson, 1971.

Thomson, J.E.P. "The Morality of Sterne's Yorick." *Journal of the Australasian Universities Language and Literature Association* 27.1 (1967): 71–8.

Toker, Leona. "Narrative Enthymeme: The Examples of Laurence Sterne and James Joyce." *Partial Answers* 4.2 (2006): 163–74.

Traugott, John. *Tristram Shandy's World: Sterne's Philosophical Rhetoric*. Berkeley: University of California Press, 1954.

Van Hammond, Lansing. *Laurence Sterne's Sermons of Mr. Yorick*. New Haven, CT: Yale University Press, 1948.

van Sant, Ann Jessie. *Eighteenth-Century Sensibility and the Novel: The Senses in Social Context*. Cambridge: Cambridge University Press, 2004.

Verestói, Anna. "The Presence of Pastoral in Sterne's Maria Scenes." *The Shandean* 20 (2009): 113–25.

Vieweg, Klaus, James Vigus, and Kathleen Wheeler, editors. *Shandean Humour in English and German Literature and Philosophy*. London: Routledge, 2013.

Virgil. *The Aeneid*. Translated by A.S. Kline. London: Poetry in Translation, 2002.

Virgil. *The Aeneid*. Translated by C. Day Lewis. Oxford: Oxford University Press, 1952.

Visser, Nicholas. "*Tristram Shandy* and the Straight Line of History." *Textual Practice* 12.3 (1998): 489–502.

Walker, Robert. "Sterne's Mummies: Fraudulent Trade in 'The Prodigal Son' Sermon." *The Scriblerian and the Kit-Cats* 50.2 (2018): 156–60.

Walsh, Marcus. "Scholarly Documentation in the Enlightenment: Validation and Interpretation." In *Ancients and Moderns in Europe: Comparative Perspectives*. Edited by Paddy Bullard and Alexis Tadie. Oxford: Voltaire Foundation, 2016, 97–112.

Walsh, Marcus, editor. *Laurence Sterne*. New York: Longman, 2002.

Walsh, Marcus. "Sterne's Slawkenbergius, the Real Presence, and the Shapeable Text." *Journal for Eighteenth-Century Studies* 17.1 (1994): 55–63.

Watkins, W.B.C. *Perilous Balance: The Tragic Genius of Swift, Johnson, and Sterne*. Princeton, NJ: Princeton University Press, 1939.

Wehrs, Donald. "Anarchic Signification and Motions of Grace in Sterne's Novelistic Satire." In *Sterne, Tristram, Yorick: Tercentenary Essays on Laurence Sterne*. Edited by Melvyn New, Peter de Voogd and Judith Hawley. Newark, NJ: University of Delaware Press, 2015, 77–99.

Wehrs, Donald. "Sterne, Cervantes, Montaigne: Fideistic Skepticism and the Rhetoric of Desire." *Comparative Literature Studies* 25.2 (1988): 127–51.

West, Robert Hunter. *The Invisible World: A Study of Pneumatology in Elizabethan Drama*. Athens: University of Georgia Press, 1939.

Westwood, Jennifer and Jacqueline Simpson. *The Penguin Book of Ghosts*. New York: Penguin, 2010.

Wetmore, Alex. *Men of Feeling in Eighteenth-Century Literature: Touching Fiction*. New York: Palgrave, 2013.

Whiskin, Margaux. *Narrative Structure and Philosophical Debates in* Tristram Shandy *and* Jacques le fataliste. London: Modern Humanities Research Association, 2014.

Whiston, William. *An Account of the Daemoniacks, and of the Power of Casting Out Daemons*. London: John Whiston, 1737.

Wilde, Oscar. "*Epistola: in carcere et vinculus.*" In *The Complete Works of Oscar Wilde*, Volume 2. Edited by Ian Small. Oxford: Oxford University Press, 2005, 35–156.

Wilde, Oscar. *The Importance of Being Earnest and Other Plays*. Edited by Peter Raby. Oxford: Oxford University Press, 1995.

Wilde, Oscar. *The Major Works*, ed. Isobel Murray. New York: Oxford University Press, 1989.

Williams, Gordon. *A Dictionary of Sexual Language and Imagery in Shakespearean and Stuart Literature*, 3 vols. New York: Athlone Press, 1994.

Williams, Helen. "Sterne's Iconography of Mourning." *Eighteenth-Century Fiction* 28.2 (2016): 313–44.

Williams, Rowan. "Theological Reading." In *The Cambridge Companion to Literature and Religion*. Edited by Susan Felch. Cambridge: Cambridge University Press, 2016, 21–34.

Wilson, James Matthew. "Confessional Reading." In *The Cambridge Companion to Literature and Religion*. Edited by Susan Felch. Cambridge: Cambridge University Press, 2016, 35–50.

Wodehouse, P.G. *Right Ho, Jeeves*. London: Barrie & Jenkins, 1978.

Wolfe, Erwin. "Falling and the Fall in *Tristram Shandy*." In *Telling Stories: Studies in Honour of Ulrich Broich*. Edited by Elmar Lehmann and Bernd Lenz. Amsterdam: Grüner, 1992, 97–108.

Wood, Ralph. *Flannery O'Connor and the Christ-Haunted South*. Grand Rapids, MI: Eerdmans, 2004.

Woolf, Virginia. *Letters of Virginia Woolf: 1923–1928*. Edited by Nigel Nicolson. New York: Harcourt Brace Jovanovich, 1975.

Woolf, Virginia. *The Common Reader, Second Series*. Edited by Andrew McNeillie. New York: Harcourt, Brace, and Jovanovich, 1984.

Young, Francis. *A History of Anglican Exorcism: Deliverance and Demonology in Church Ritual*. London: I.B. Tauris, 2018.

Zimmerman, Everett. "*Tristram Shandy* and Narrative Representation." *The Eighteenth Century* 28.2 (1987): 127–47.

Zwaneveld, Agnes Maria. *A Bookseller's Hobby-Horse and the Rhetoric of Translation: Anthony Ernst Munnikhuisen and Bernardus Brunius and the First Dutch Edition of* Tristram Shandy *(1776–1779)*. Amsterdam: Rodopi, 1996.

Index

Abaddon 21
Abbess of Andoüillets 9–10, 37, 79
Abbott, Bud 30
Abdera 88
Abelard, Peter 14
Abishag the Shunammite 56–7
abolition 3–4
Abraham 73, 132n.34
Achilles 104
Adam 20, 34, 102
adultery 3, 13, 26, 32–3, 60–3, 108–10
Aeneas 73
Ahaziah 16–17
Alexander of Pheres 95
allegory 12, 84, 86, 108–9, 125n.51, 132n.54
ambience 15, 37, 64, 77, 92
American Beauty 58
angels 17–19, 22, 90, 107
anthropophagi 99
Antichrist 9
Aphrodite 99–100
aposiopesis 7
Aristophanes 34
Aristotle 89
Ark of the Covenant 119n.2
association of ideas 32
astral plane 76–7, 90
atheism 5, 14, 73, 91–2, 114
Atlantis 60
atmosphere 73–6, 84, 92, 105
Auden, W.H. 60
aura 64, 77, 92

Baal 34–5
Bacchus 54
baculum 2
Barnabas 21
Bathsheba 64, 132n.54

Battestin, Martin 14
Beatrice 88
Beauties of Sterne 17, 47, 53, 57
Bedlam 37
Beelzebub 16–17
Beersheba 109
Beguine Nurse 76
Berra, Yogi 7
Bevoriskius 102
Bierce, Ambrose 40–1, 98
Big Lebowski 49
black page 21–3
blank page 21, 24–6, 37
blush 17–19, 78
Boaz 51, 63–4, 76
Boswell, James 11
Botticelli, Sandro 90
Boulogne 99
Boyle, Robert 12
breeches 22, 34
Breughel 105
Browne, Thomas 12
Buffy the Vampire Slayer 89
Bunyan, John 108
Burton, Robert 1, 24, 44, 83–4
busybodies 3, 38–9, 113

Calvinism 24
Canaanites 50
cant 35–7
captive 100
Carter, George 49
Cash, Arthur 4–5, 34, 72
casuistry 37, 85
cathedrals 104
celibacy 26
Cervantes 1, 48, 79–81, 102, 111
chambermaids 31–2, 66, 84–5, 101, 109
Chambers, Ephraim 56

Chaucer, Geoffrey 126n.68
Chesterton, G.K. 68, 96, 123n.22
chestnuts 118
chocolate 45, 77
circumcision 82
Clarke, Samuel 43
Cleland, John 68
Cockfield, Joseph 3
coitus interruptus 50, 65
Coleridge, Samuel Taylor 10
concession 46
concubines 14, 38–9, 46
conscience 17, 25, 33–5, 48, 60, 67, 110
conversation 41, 57
Costello, Lou 30
country folk 19, 40, 54, 74, 105–6, 118
Cowper, William 21
Cross, Wilbur 22, 83
Cupid 88
cuttlefish rhetoric 22

damsels 56–7, 101
Dan 109
dancing 19, 40, 54, 68, 105, 118
Dante 27, 88
David 49, 56, 62, 76, 95–6, 132n.54
Day, W.G. 48, 130n.2
de Botton, Alain 114
de Cordouè, Ferdinand 9
Dee, John 80
Deeds 17–18
Defoe, Daniel 90–1
Dekker, Thomas 52–3
de la Casa, John 15
demons 2–3, 6–7, 9–28, 43, 84, 87, 99, 113
de Voogd, Peter 54, 79, 125n.51
devotions 60, 103, 114, 133–4n.64
d'Holbach, Baron 14, 31, 73
Dido 64, 73, 88
Dionysius 54
Don Juan 34

Don Quixote 79, 81, 102, 111
doppelganger 108
d'Orleans 49
double entendre 1–3, 39, 52, 57, 68–9, 71, 78, 83, 104
Draper, Eliza 32, 75
dreams 11, 19, 38, 58, 68, 76, 80, 84, 110
Dr. Eustace 87
Dr. Slop 16, 36
dryads 54
Dryden, John 137n.53
dualism 85
Dürer, Albrecht 64
Dussinger, John 48

Earl of Clonmell 53
Eastern Orthodoxy 73
ectoplasm 75
Eden 24
Ekron 16
Elijah 29, 34–5, 39, 87, 95, 128n.31
Eliot, T.S. 4, 44, 90
Elisha 2, 64
Eliza 60–3, 66, 75–6, 80, 88, 95, 103, 108–10
Elysian Fields 99
Enlightenment 1, 11–12, 89
enthusiasm 35–6
enthymemes 37
epexegesis 40
Epictetus 119n.2
epitaph 22–4
Er 50
Ernulphus 16
erostesis 33
Esau 31–2
etcetera 53, 65
Eugenius 95
euphemisms 2–3, 52–3, 104
Eupheus 116
Euripides 88, 95
Eve 34
exorcism 6, 10–11, 15, 28

Fairyland 90
fauns 54
Ferguson, Robert 23
fideism 34
Fielding, Henry 64, 87–9, 137n.53
Finknottle, Gussie 40
Fitzgerald, Percy 29, 39
Fludd, Robert 22
flying saints 92
Foley, Robert 77–9
forceps 20, 36
Forster, E.M. 20–1
Fort Pitt 42
Fourmantel, Catherine 32
Franciscans 106–7
Franklin, Benjamin 42
French Officer 94–5
fundamentalism 1

genealogy 73, 103
genius 6, 30, 42, 46, 57, 68, 81
Gerard, W.B. 29–30
German 65–6, 100
Ghost of Christmas Present 99
ghosts 7, 10, 12, 73–111
Gilead 69
Glanvill, Joseph 91
gloves 83, 96–8
gluttony of delicacy 99
Gnosticism 7, 77
goats 32, 47–9, 51, 53–5, 62, 69, 113
goblins 12, 83
Goethe 4
golden calves 109
Gomer 64, 108–9
Goodhue, Elizabeth 72
Good Samaritan 58, 69, 95, 100, 115
gothic fiction 10, 89
Gow, James 44
grace 18, 20, 24, 28, 105–7, 110, 113
Grand Tour 40
graveyards 22, 80–1
gravity 10, 28, 118
Gray, Thomas 29, 102

Great Instauration 20
Griffiths, Ralph 3, 53
grisette 66, 83, 97–8

Hall-Stevenson, John 13, 33
Hamlet's ghost 73, 75–6, 83, 88, 97
Hammond, Lansing 45
Harries, Elizabeth 25
Hawthorne, Nathaniel 96, 129n.43
Heaven 7, 17–20, 41, 73, 75, 78, 86, 99, 101, 106, 111
Hector 104
Hell 7, 10–11, 15, 18–20, 23, 28, 78, 86, 105
Hercules 96
historicism 115–16
historiography 93, 101–5
Hobbes, Thomas 11
hobbyhorses 116
Hogarth, William 57, 68
Holland, William 53
Hollis, Thomas 52
Homenas 43
Homer 44
horses 2, 79, 89
Hosea 64, 108–9
Hume, David 4, 12, 31
humility 35
hypocrisy 23, 35, 110–11, 126n.60

iatrochemistry 134n.65
iconography 21–6, 45, 64, 76, 109
I Love Lucy 45
Imago Dei 104
incubus 83–4
innocent entendre 53
Isaac 31–2
Israel 16, 50, 76, 108–9
itinerant stage 36

Jack, Ian 102
Jacob 2, 31–2, 51
James, Anne 80
James, William 80
Jefferson, Thomas 4, 46

Jenny 15, 19–20, 111
Jesus Christ 7, 19–20, 23, 26, 64, 87, 96, 101, 115
   exorcist 14–15, 126n.69
   genealogy 48–9, 76, 103
   parables 78, 100
   satire 110
Jezebel 2
John Paul II 1
Johnson, Samuel 7–8
Joseph 50
Joyce, James 22, 90
Judah 6, 48–54, 59, 65–7, 113
Juvenal 98

Kames, Lord 11
Kelly, Edward 80
Keymer, Thomas 48, 52, 72
Killigrew, Thomas 53
King Arthur 88
King James Bible 34, 51, 56, 114
Knox, Vicemus 3, 63
Kraft, Elizabeth 5, 44, 47, 71, 109

Laban 31
Lady Wrestler 2
La Fleur 53, 55, 65, 81–2
Lanham, Richard 116
Laputa 23
Last Judgment 25
laughter 7, 11, 23, 25, 29, 77, 111
laundry 104
Lazarus 40
Leah 31–3, 113
Leavis, Frank 117–18
Le Fever 15, 17–19
Leibniz, Gottfried 85
Lessius 20
Levirate marriage 50
Levites 14, 38
Lewis, Albert 117
Lewis, C.S. 46, 69, 78, 86, 92, 116–18
libertines 33
Lincoln, Abraham 4, 100
liturgy 11

Locke, John 6, 9, 32
logical positivism 1
Lombardy 58
Lorenzo 101, 104–7
Lot 51
Louvre 101
Lucian 24, 87, 101
Lumley, Elizabeth 32
lust 26, 34–5, 60
Luther, Martin 10, 20–1
Lynch, David 73–4
Lyttleton, Lord 87

Machiavelli 95
Macksey, Richard 94
Madame de L*** 66
Madame de L— 109–10
Madame de V— 86
madness 11, 37, 97
Magdalene, Mary 64, 126n.69
magic 21, 71, 76, 80, 87–8, 90
Magritte, René 74
malice 21
man-machine 73, 86, 106
Mano, Keith 117–18
marbled page 21, 23–4, 126n.60
Maria of Moulins 6, 47–69, 73, 83, 85
Marquis de Sade 48
Marvell, Andrew 52
masks 71–2, 83
masturbation 33–4, 48–50, 64–5, 131n.30
materialism 12, 77–8, 85–6, 91–2
McGlynn, Paul 48, 62
mechanical philosophy 77–8, 83
meekness 105, 114
memento mori 23–4, 81
memory 17–18, 20, 44, 75–6
Mencken, H.L. 38
merkins 32–3, 59
metaphor 13, 56, 62, 69, 80, 84, 113
metonym 39–40, 60–1, 96–7, 109
Miller, Samuel 3
Milton, John 10
miracles 12, 77, 97, 123n.22

mirth 4, 25, 37–8, 42, 46, 93, 100, 118
Moabites 51, 76, 103
Modern Venus 74
Momus 24, 110
monism 85
Montague, Elizabeth 87
Montpellier 79
monuments 74, 101, 103
Moorfields 37
More, Thomas 6, 22, 114
Moses 19, 87
Moulin Rouge 109
mourning 10, 26, 100
Mrs. Grundy 3, 40
Mrs. Shandy 2, 16, 93–8
Mulholland Drive 73
Mulligan, Spike 22
Mundungus 99

Nampont 64–6, 100
Nanette 19, 40, 54, 105, 118
Nathan 62, 95, 132n.54
necromancy 87–8
New, Melvyn 5, 17, 27, 29, 37, 44–5, 48, 72, 79, 115
Newton, Isaac 12
New Yorker 62, 78
Nietzsche, Friedrich 4, 92, 114
No Exit 20
non finito 25
noses 2, 15, 32, 36, 76
nostalgia 7, 73–4, 81, 90
Notre Dame 104
nuns 9, 37, 76, 79
Nurnberg Chronicle 25

Obed 76
obscenity 1–3, 38, 48, 57, 68
obsession 11
O'Connor, Flannery 8
Odysseus 67, 88
Onan 49–50, 64–5
Ophelia 64
original sin 24, 68

Paidagunes 44
Palace Royal 101
Pangloss 58
Paraleipomenon 39, 102
Pardons 101
Paris 81–4, 99, 105
Parker, Matthew 24
Parnell, Tim 72, 115–16
paromologia 46
Parson Tickletext 64
Parthenon 99
Pascal, Blaise 34
paternity 16, 54, 93–4, 96–8
pathos 39, 42, 49, 57, 60
Patrides, C.A. 25
penis 2, 32, 36, 76
Pentateuch 2
Pentecost 36, 109
Perenas 79
Perseus 88
Peter 96
Pharez 51
Pharisees 23, 100, 106
Piedmontese Lady 31–2, 109
pilgrimage 41, 59, 65–6, 100
plagiarism 42–5
plain style 1
Plato 77–8
Pope, Alexander 24
pornography 1, 38, 48, 57, 68
possession 11–13
postsecularism 141n.7
pragmatism 95
pregnancy 6, 48–51, 54, 65
Presbyterians 3
preternatural 9–11, 14–15, 80
pride 20, 25–6, 28, 45
principalities 6, 10
Prior, Matthew 24
Prodigal Son 40, 59, 96, 115
projection 66
prostitution 7, 32–3, 46–69, 107, 109
Proust, Marcel 90
prudery 38
psychoanalysis 83, 86

psychophysical parallelism 85
Purgatory 73, 88, 91, 114
Puritans 38, 108
Purton, Valarie 47–8, 57

Quakers 35
Queen of Navarre 65
Quintilian 101

Rabelais 1–2, 22, 29, 36, 39–40, 48, 81
Rachel 31–2
Rahab 64
Raphael 101
rationalism 1
Read, Herbert 5
religious turn 141n.7
reliquary 103
resurrection 71, 80, 88, 136n.25
revelation 81, 97–8
Richardson, Samuel 64
riddles 10, 49, 73, 93
Romantics 92
Rome 58, 99, 101
Rose, William 39
Ruffhead, Owen 42–3
Ruth 51, 63–4, 76–7, 103

sacraments 29, 37, 41, 114
Sadducism 91
Saint Booger 54
Saint James Shrine 65–6
Saint Peter's Basilica 58
Samuel 87
Sancho Panza 102–3
Satan 3, 6, 9–28
Saul 87
sausage 2
Savoy 58
Schedel, Hartmann 25
scholasticism 20
Schopenhauer, Arthur 4
Screwtape 7, 99
séance 21, 76, 87
secularism 14, 29, 141n.7
self-deception 14, 17, 34, 67, 96, 110

self-examination 24–6, 107, 110
Sensorium 96
sentimentality 17–18, 48, 53–4
Septuagint 2, 103
sepulchers 23–4, 33
Shaftsbury 29
Shakespeare 1, 27, 117
 Comedy of Errors 60-1
 Hamlet 10, 23, 64, 73–7, 81, 83, 88, 97
 Macbeth 10, 61, 90
 Much Ado about Nothing 7, 53, 68–9
Shelah 50, 56
Shua 50
Shunammite Woman 2, 64
signets 51, 54–5
single entendre 1, 57
Sirens 67
skepticism 12–13, 91–2
Slawkenbergius, Hafen 76
Smelfungus 99
snuffbox 103, 107
solipsism 104
South, Robert 36
sparrows 102
spleen 38, 99–100
squires 102–3
starling 4, 100
Stedmond, John 72
Stevenson, John Allen 113
stoicism 114
Stout, Gardiner 83, 108
stream-of-consciousness 90
Swift, Jonathan 1, 87–8
 Gulliver's Travels 23, 40, 105
 Tale of a Tub 19, 37, 77–8, 85
Sylvio 47, 66, 134n.65
Sylvius, Franciscus 134n.65

Tamar 6, 48–69
Tartuffe 12, 23, 32–3
teleportation 76, 90, 97
theosis 7, 73–4, 86, 93, 108, 114
theosophy 11, 76, 84

Thesaurus Exorcismorum 10
Tickletoby 2
Tinmath 59
tobacco 103, 106–7
Toby 15–19, 73, 85
Tolstoy, Leo 26
Tom 2
tombs 22–4, 107, 125n.51
tomes 23–4
Transfiguration 87, 101
Traugott, John 29
travel writing 40, 66, 93–5, 99–102, 108
Trim 22, 76
Tristrapedia 20

Uriah 64

vagina 2, 50, 52
Valet 40
veils 22–3, 48, 51, 69, 82, 94, 125n.51
Venus de Medici 99
Virgil 64
Virgin Mary 64
Voltaire 58

Walpole, Horace 10, 89
Walter 12–13, 16, 22, 37, 85, 94, 117
Warburton, William 10, 19, 46
Wedgwood, Joseph 47
Wesley, John 3
whiskers 65
Whiston, William 12
Whyte, D. 3
Widow of Zarephath 29, 39
Widow Wadman 16, 25, 37
Wife of Bath 126n.68
Wilberforce, William 4
Wilde, Oscar 5, 22, 59, 113
Witch of Endor 80, 87
Wodehouse, P.G. 40
Woman at the Well 64
Woman in the Wilderness 64
Woolf, Virginia 4, 90, 104
work of redemption 83

Yahweh 16
Young Frankenstein 89
Young Goodman Brown 3, 107–8

zigzaggery 10, 54